The Logic of Comparative Social Inquiry

The Logic of Comparative Social Inquiry

ADAM PRZEWORSKI
University of Chicago

HENRY TEUNE
University of Pennsylvania

ROBERT E. KRIEGER PUBLISHING COMPANY
MALABAR, FLORIDA

Original Edition   1970
Reprint   1982

Printed and Published by
ROBERT E. KRIEGER PUBLISHING COMPANY, INC.
KRIEGER DRIVE
MALABAR, FLORIDA 32950

Copyright © 1970, by
JOHN WILEY & SONS, INC.
Reprinted by Arrangement

Printed in the United States of America

Library of Congress Cataloging in Publication Data

Przeworski, Adam.
    The logic of comparative social inquiry.

    Reprint. Originally published: New York : Wiley
Interscience, 1970.
    Bibliography: p.
    Includes index.
    1. Social sciences—Research. I. Teune,
Henry. II. Title.
[H62.P79 1982]   300'.72   81-19332
ISBN 0-89874-462-8   AACR2

10   9   8   7   6   5   4

*To our collaborators in
the International Studies
of Values in Politics*

PREFACE

The ideas presented in this book developed during the course of our participation in a comparative research project, the International Studies of Values in Politics, which was a study of the relationship between characteristics of local political leadership and the behavior of local governments in India, Poland, the United States, and Yugoslavia. It is to our colleagues in this research venture, with whom we worked face-to-face for a number of years, that we dedicate this book.

Among the first problems we confronted were those of measurement. In the fall of 1965 the first pretest of value-scale items was under way. The goal of the pretest was to develop valid and reliable scales of values in four national samples. Before the data were gathered we anticipated extreme difficulty in identifying a set of items that would form satisfactory scales of the same values in all four countries. In our discussions we formulated the idea of constructing scales from a combination of international items, which would ensure cross-national reliability, and national items, which would contribute to validity in each country. Using different items for each country, however, could be justified only if the items were shown to be "equivalent." This procedure was subsequently developed and published as "Equivalence in Cross-National Research" (*Public Opinion Quarterly,* Winter 1966). At that time we cast our arguments in terms of constructing scales in cross-national research. We did not fully comprehend the generality of our arguments for any type of comparative research and the epistemological assumptions of such measurement procedures.

The second problem we had to face arose from the need to obtain "comparable" measures of community "activeness" in four countries. The data that could be used to assess "activeness" were outside the control of the researchers. In fact there was not a single item of data that was the same in all four countries. Our previous arguments had to be modified and generalized.

But the most important problem was to translate the data that were being gathered into a form amenable to theoretical statements. Were we to be content with statements such as "in India . . . , but in Poland . . ."? The data were accumulated at three levels: individual political leaders, local governments, and countries. The question was one of what phenomena should be explained by what. We felt that comparative research should focus on *within-systems relationships* rather than attributes of systems. This idea had far-reaching implications for our thinking and perhaps was the key to assembling our thoughts for writing this book.

Although these ideas would never have been developed without an opportunity to confront problems of comparative research, the International Studies of Values in Politics should not be identified with the views propounded in this book. We intend a general treatment of the logic of comparative research free from the operations and findings of any particular research program. The intellectual orientation of the book is based in our belief that methodological procedures should rely on explicit epistemology. In our view the weakness of books on logic of inquiry is that they are usually written with little understanding of the practical problems and limitations of research. If such philosophy of science books are understood and taken literally, research is likely to be paralyzed. By contrast, many books on techniques of research are so involved in presenting specific procedures and techniques that neither their justifications nor their implications are discussed. Only if tied to epistemological assumptions can specific research procedures be evaluated on intellectual grounds rather than in terms of vague criteria of utility or lore about difficulty. We have made a self-conscious attempt to link specific procedures of research to at least one philosophical context of inquiry. In this sense this book is "balanced." We did not, however, achieve a balance between "logic" and "procedure" for each point made. We appreciate that we do not fully understand the procedural implications of some of our logical points nor the epistemological assumptions of some of the recommended procedures. This is principally a "how to do it" book in which techniques and procedures are set in meta-methodological context. It is not a general philosophical treatise, and actually our excursions into the philosophical realm are dictated directly by the technical problems considered.

We think this book is written at a propitious time in the development of the social sciences. Since the 1950s the dominant approach to the study of "other cultures" has been represented by area study programs. Hundreds of millions of dollars have been invested in the study of predetermined sets of data—Latin America, Africa, South Asia. In the 1960s the results of several large-scale social and political research projects began to enter the domain of the social sciences—Almond and Verba, Cantril, Inkeles, and others. Although the area study approaches are justified both in terms of scientific results and also by political, social, and educational benefits accruing to society, their value for general social theory is less obvious than the value derived from general cross-national or cross-cultural studies. Most of these general studies, however, have accepted a methodology validated by social science practice in a single culture, particularly the United States. They have tended to view the problems of comparative research in terms of research difficulties, such as translating questionnaires, training interviewers, assuring accuracy of data, and have tended to ignore the insight of the area specialist: a nation, culture, or region must be considered as a "whole."

The contrast between the approaches represented by area-focused and general comparative studies should not be overdrawn. What is of greater importance are two changes taking place among social scientists. The first is an increased awareness of the nature and importance of theory, accompanied by the understanding that data acquire meaning only within theoretical contexts. We see a growing concern about the formal structure of theories and a growing emphasis on theoretical formulation of research. This emphasis on theory and the de-emphasis on gathering and analyzing unstructured data is, we think, the important issue for social science in the 1970s. Although the "data revolution" is not yet over, the advent of formal theory will revolutionize social science anew.

The second change is the emergence of competent social scientists throughout the world. No Latin American study program in a North American university can match the detailed information, language skills, and access to data possessed by the hundreds of Latin American social scientists. Comparative studies can now enlist the efforts of social scientists everywhere and can mobilize more knowledge and effort on a particular problem than a single foreign scholar could ever hope to achieve in a lifetime. The logic of comparative research presented in this book, we believe, is congruent with these changes in social science.

The ideas contained in this book were jointly developed over a number of years of argument and discussion. When several ideas took shape, we decided to write a book. This decision compelled us to rethink several of our basic tenets and to form new ones. Przeworski took responsibility for drafting Part One, and Teune accepted responsibility for Part Two. We jointly rewrote every sentence and paragraph and jointly assume responsibility for the whole.

Several people have made direct contributions to this book. John Sprague of Washington University zealously wrote several pages of com-

ments on the drafts. Raymond Boudon of the Sorbonne, Raoul Narrol of
the University of Buffalo, and Glaucio Soares of the Facultad Latinoameri-
cana de Cencias Sociales pointed out several specific problems. The draft
manuscript was reviewed by several publishers who provided us with
anonymous comments, some of which we found very helpful. One of the
readers who identified himself was Fred Frey of the Massachusetts Institute
of Technology.

What started as a technical discussion of a measurement technique grew
into a "frontal attack," to cite one of the reviewers, on the problems of
comparative research. We are well aware that this is by no means the last
word on this topic. On the contrary, many problems are treated here in
an introductory manner. Our hope is that we have formulated some
problems in a way amenable to systematic discussion and to the development
of solutions.

Because we have been told so often that this is a controversial book, we
now almost believe it. But, in our view, it is no more controversial than
the logic of inquiry from which we drew unorthodox conclusions to fit the
reality of comparative research.

Adam Przeworski
August 1969   *Henry Teune*

The Logic of Comparative Social Inquiry

INTRODUCTION

An Overview of Problems

The purpose of this book is to identify problems encountered in one area of social scientific inquiry and to offer some solutions to them. But the identification of problems is not independent of the proposed solutions: both are based on a set of assumptions about the accepted goals and the postulated model of inquiry. Since the study of societies lies at the crossroad of several models of science, these assumptions are of crucial importance. The controversies concerning methodological and technical strategies in comparative research often stem from disagreements about underlying assumptions rather than from differences in the evaluation of the "propriety" of these strategies vis-à-vis an agreed set of postulates. Only the latter type of controversies can be resolved in the course of logical analysis. Controversies concerning the choice of the basic postulates of science require explication of underlying metascientific criteria and are usually unsolvable. Thus the question whether physics should be concerned with the measurement of gravity or with actions of angels is largely an issue of historical scale and intellectually only partially debatable, whereas the question whether sitting under an apple tree is the best way to measure gravity can be fairly well decided. The question whether history should be concerned with every moment in the life of George Washington or with the role of elites in national revolutions is again unresolvable, but the question of how to determine whether George Marshall's report on the life of Washington is a reliable source can be answered more easily. Indeed, if some basic postulates are accepted, the question of measuring the seraphim's superiority over the cherubim is an easier one to solve than the problem of whether attitudes "can" be measured.

Since different models of science persist within and between various branches of the study of society, an attempt will be made to state some

3

assumptions of the set of recommendations that will be presented. The extent to which we are aware of these assumptions is most certainly incomplete, but hopefully even a partial explication will increase the intelligibility of the problems and the recommended solutions.

Some Assumptions of Comparative Research

The pivotal assumption of this analysis is that social science research, including comparative inquiry, should and can lead to general statements about social phenomena. This assumption implies that human or social behavior can be explained in terms of general laws established by observation. Introduced here as an expression of preference, this assumption will not be logically justified.

It is this kind of assumption that accompanied the development of comparative inquiry during the last two centuries. The corollary of this assumption is that social behavior conforms to a limited number of recognizable patterns. One of the major patterns identified by social scientists such as Comte, Marx, Durkheim, Weber, and Spencer is that societies undergo a structured process of development.

Contemporary cross-societal inquiries share many of the perspectives and assumptions of these thinkers, particularly inquiries that combine comparative and developmental approaches. Whether explicit or implicit, developmental assumptions underlie much of the current cross-cultural research. Are mobility rates in developed societies higher or lower than in less developed societies? Is the political culture of "modern" political systems more "participatory" than that in "traditional" systems? Is recruitment to social roles based on the same criteria in traditional and modern societies?

The combination of comparative and developmental perspectives is largely a consequence of the social milieu of contemporary social sciences and, logically, they need not be combined. We can very well imagine a study of Ceylon, Poland, or the United States that is devoid of developmental assumptions. We read studies not about Ceylon, however, but about "the case of" Ceylon, Poland, or the United States as illustrations of developmental processes taking place in different places and at different times.[1] It is also important to realize that any description—any descriptive comparative statement—of a particular social situation as a "case" is based on

[1] W. H. Wriggins, "Implements to Unity in a New Nation: The Case of Ceylon," *American Political Science Review,* 55, 1961; Zygmunt Bauman, "Economic Development, Social Structure, and Elite Formation: The Case of Poland," in J. J. Wiatr, ed., *Studies in the Polish Political System,* Ossolineum, Wroclaw, 1967.

some theory that treats the particular social system at least as a confirming or disconfirming illustration. Even ostensibly descriptive historical studies of particular social systems or institutions often assume a whole set of general theoretical statements.

Nomothetic versus Idiographic Approaches

The orientation in the social sciences toward statements of a theoretical nature has been and remains a subject of controversy in various disciplines. Historians argued whether their approach should be idiographic or nomothetic;[2] anthropologists discussed whether functionally integrated systems must be treated only in toto or whether traits can be abstracted and compared;[3] sociologists continue to disagree about the importance of the "postulate of indispensability"[4]—whether every existing structure is functional for the system; economists argued whether a universal definition of their discipline can be constructed;[5] and political scientists debated the value of generalizations confined to a specific set of institutions.[6]

Although the traditional juxtaposition of the "idiographic" and "nomothetic" sciences has lost much of its edge, many of the problems currently discussed are still classifiable within these terms. Social sciences grew out of philosophy, particularly the philosophy of history, and repercussions from the traditional controversies can still be felt. These controversies concern the model of inquiry that is best applicable to social reality and the status of general statements in the social sciences. Aron reconstructs this age-old controversy in the following manner:

"Historical science is no more the mere reproduction of that which has been than natural science is the reproduction of nature. . . . But though history, like natural science, is a reconstruction, it is a reconstruction of a

[2] Hans Meyerhoff, ed., *The Philosophy of History in Our Time,* Doubleday, New York, 1959; Louis Gottschalk, ed., *Generalizations in the Writing of History,* University of Chicago Press, Chicago, 1963.

[3] See the discussion between Radcliffe-Brown and Lowie concerning the utility of the concept of function. Particularly, A. R. Radcliffe-Brown, "On the Concept of Function in the Social Sciences," *American Anthropologist,* 42, 1940.

[4] R. K. Merton, *Social Theory and Social Structure,* Free Press, New York, 1957; S. M. Lipset, *Political Man,* Doubleday, New York, 1960, Methodological Appendix to Chapter One.

[5] For a summary see N. J. Smelser, "Notes on the Methodology of Comparative Analysis of Economic Activity," *Social Science Information,* 6, 1967.

[6] R. C. Macridis, *The Study of Comparative Government,* Doubleday, New York, 1955; G. A. Almond, "Comparative Political Systems," *Journal of Politics,* 18, 1956; Harry Eckstein, "A Prespective on Comparative Politics, Past and Present," in Harry Eckstein and David Apter, eds., *Comparative Politics,* Free Press, New York, 1963.

very different type. The ultimate aim of natural science is a systematized complex of laws. . . . The ultimate subject of history is a unique series of events. . . . Natural science seeks for law, history for the particular."[7]

Nagel notes the same difference:

"Even a cursory examination of treatises in theoretical natural science and of books on history reveals the prima facie difference between them, that by and large the statements of the former are general in form, and contain few if any references to specific objects, places, times, whereas the statements of the latter are almost without exception singular and replete with proper names, dates, and geographic specifications. To this extent, at least the alleged contrast between the natural sciences as nomothetic and history as idiographic appears to be well founded."[8]

If this distinction is accepted, the form of statements in natural sciences is "whenever and wherever X occurs, X is in a certain relation to Y," whereas the form of social science statements specifies a spatio-temporal location and makes all subsequent propositions relative to these parameters. Natural science statements say that "a particle to which no force is applied will be moving with constant velocity in a straight line," whereas social sciences are required to state that "in Africa during the early 1960's ethnically based parties entered situations of violent conflict." A statement specifying that particles are moving in a straight line in Africa is true, but redundant, because particles move in the same way everywhere and at all times. A statement generalizing that "political systems in which all parties are ethnically based are unstable" is judged to be "improper" because parties do not behave in a universal fashion. Statements of a general nature are thus meaningless because they involve concepts that are excessively general and violate the specific features of each social system. The main argument against the possibilities of nomothetic statements concerning social reality stems from the observation that such statements are never universally true; even if they appear to be true, they are meaningless insofar as they are based on general concepts that "do violence" to the specific features of each social system. The controversy thus concerns (1) the nature of general theoretical statements in the social sciences and (2) the nature of standardized observations of social phenomena across cultures.

Why are general statements concerning social reality not universally true? Some of the possible reasons may stem from the errors of measurement in the observed variables, a problem also encountered in the natural sciences.

[7] Raymond Aron, "Relativism in History," in Hans Meyerhoff, ed., *op cit.,* p. 157.
[8] Ernst Nagel, "The Logic of Historical Analysis," in Hans Meyerhoff, ed., *op. cit.,* pp. 203-204.

Another reason is that selected sets of social variables are rarely autonomous; there are always other factors that can influence any observed relationship. An individual's political participation is not completely determined by the level of education; its extent is influenced by many more factors. Frustration is not the sole predictor of aggression, and mutual perception of husband and wife is not the sole predictor of marital success. Two interpretations of this incomplete determination of social phenomena are possible, and they are of crucial importance for general social science theory.

In one interpretation, the incompleteness of a factorial system (system of variables) is the only reason for indetermination: *if all relevant factors were known,* then the same multivariate statement would yield a deterministic explanation regardless of time and space. This kind of an interpretation constitutes a direct transference of the dominant natural science model to the study of social reality. If all factors leading to aggressive behaviors were known, then a multivariate statement would explain aggression wherever and whenever it occurs. This view of social reality implies a certain research strategy that, thus far, no one has followed: research conducted on random samples of the world population, regardless of the social systems to which individuals, groups, or subsystems belong. Social science based on this kind of assumption would be a priori a-historical: historical circumstances in which particular observations were made would be ignored since they are assumed to have no significance. This kind of model of social science is implicit in the writings of some psychologists and was actually postulated by Malewski as the proper model for constructing general theories of behavior.[9] If this model is accepted, there can be no bridge between theoretical and historical social science. Theoretical statements would be formulated in terms devoid of proper names of social systems, whereas historical statements would include such names. In the second interpretation, social science statements cannot be universally true because the interaction of various characteristics within each social system creates unique, or at least varying, patterns of determination relative to each social system. Therefore the identification of the social system in which a given phenomenon occurs is a part of its explanation. In the extreme version of this position no general statements applicable across social systems are possible, and all social science statements must be confined to particular social systems. In a less extreme version, probably dominant within political science today, social science statements are relative to classes of nations or "areas" that share syndromes of historical, cultural, and social characteristics. Thus one can

[9] A. Malewski, "Dwa Modele Socjologii" (Two Models of Sociology), *Studia Socjologiczne,* **1,** 1961.

make general statements concerning Latin America, Southeast Asia, Eastern Europe, but statements of a more general nature are improper.

The assumptions underlying the choice of either model of social science are of an empirical nature: they concern the most likely pattern of determination of social phenomena. In one view, it is more likely that this determination of social phenomena is sufficiently general to warrant an a priori abstraction from spatiotemporal parameters. In the other view, the determination is expected to be highly specific to particular social systems or groups of social systems so that the generality of statements concerning social reality is inherently limited. One can expect that the validity of either of these perspectives is relative to the nature of phenomena under investigation as well as the state of knowledge. The ahistorical assumptions are probably more valid with regard to psychological processes, whereas relativistic assumptions may turn out to be more valid in explaining social and cultural behavior. As long as these assumptions are explicit, further development of comparative inquiry will gradually provide information on their validity.

Systems versus Variables in Comparative Research

In our view, the crux of the problem lies in the status of the proper names of social systems within general theory. What does it mean that observations of social reality are relative to particular social units? The real difference between this assumption and the one disregarding social relativism is that particular social units are treated as *predictors,* in the same manner as variables are used as predictors in general theories. The status of social units, however, is not the same as the status of variables. It is not immediately clear why the identification of a particular social unit predicts a given social phenomenon. The relationship between education and political participation may be different in Latin America and Asia, and consequently the knowledge that this relationship is observed in a certain area yields a gain in prediction of political participation.

The goal of comparative research is to substitute names of variables for the names of social systems, such as Ghana, the United States, Africa, or Asia. To use first an example from the natural sciences, suppose that a group of physicists identified the temperature at which water boils in New York. Another group conducted the same research in Denver, and the results obviously turned out to be different. An idiographically oriented physicist would naturally conclude that all we can do is to describe New York and Denver in terms of the temperature of boiling water. But other physicists would replace the spatial parameter by a variable. They would state that the temperature of boiling depends upon atmospheric pressure and would disregard other characteristics of New York and Denver. When medical scholars discovered that the rate of heart attacks is lower in Japan than in the United States, they too replaced the names of social systems by a variable, arguing that the incidence of such attacks depends upon the consumption of polysaturated fats. This role of comparative studies in the social sciences was formulated by Bendix, Suchman, and Ossowski. Bendix describes comparative analysis in general terms:

"Comparative sociological studies represent an attempt to develop concepts and generalizations at a level between what is true of all societies and what is true of one society at one point in time and space."[10]

He discusses the process of "urbanization" in India and, in noting the difference between India and some other countries, proceeds to ask whether this difference stems from either the fact that the country studied is "India" or that it is a country at a different level of economic development. In other words, the level of economic development may be substituted for the name of a specific social system, "India." Both Ossowski and Suchman posit this role of comparative research in very explicit terms. Ossowski classifies theoretical propositions on the basis of their level of generality:

"The category of statement with the highest scope introduces cultural variables. It thus includes generalizations concerning behavior of persons remaining under the influence of a given culture or cultures and does not extend to all societies. The second category includes those generalizations from which the *cultural variable has been eliminated by international comparative research* [emphasis added] or those in which it was not taken into account because of a previously accepted assumption that culture does not influence this type of phenomena."[11]

Finally, in Suchman's view:

"Thus, comparative studies which deal with two or more different groups at different times might most meaningfully be viewed in terms of generalizations, explanations, and predictions *where the time and space factors are incorporated as control variables into the statement of the generalization itself.*"[12]

[10] Reinhard Bendix, "Concepts and Generalizations in Comparative Sociological Studies," *American Sociological Review,* **28**, 1963, p. 532.
[11] S. Ossowski, "Zoologia Spoleczna i Zronznicowani Kulturowe" (Social Zoology and the Differentiation of Culture), *Studia Socjologiczne,* 1963, p. 5. (Translated by the authors.)
[12] E. A. Suchman, "The Comparative Method in Social Research," *Rural Sociology,* **29**, 1964, p. 129.

Although particular social systems do influence the nature of observed relationships and do yield a gain in prediction, it will be argued here that, if some additional assumptions are accepted, proper names can be replaced by variables in the course of comparative research. Nomothetic statements can be made.

Another set of objections against general, theoretical statements about social reality stems from the argument that social phenomena are unique, or at least vary, from one social system to another. Therefore if the same general concepts are applied to phenomena observed in different social systems, the specific features of these phenomena are disregarded. This argument is often based on reification of concepts. In the strong ontological version it is sometimes said that social phenomena are "not comparable" as if it were the nature of social reality rather than a property of statements made about reality that is being disputed. Social phenomena do not have a property of "being comparable" or "not comparable." "Comparability" depends upon the level of generality of the language that is applied to express observations. The response to the classical objection to comparing "apples and oranges" is simple: they are "fruits." And the answer to the question whether there are interest groups in the Soviet Union depends upon the level of generality of the concept "interest group." If interest groups are defined as "formalized groups aware of common interests and exerting pressure on a government to consider these interests," then some countries may have few interest groups. But if "pressure" is dropped from the definition, the number of interest groups will be related to the level of functional specialization in a society, and one could speak about "pressure interest groups" and "mobilizing interest groups" as two types of the same phenomenon differing by the relative amounts of communication that they transmit up and down the political system.

In this strong version, the argument is based on a misunderstanding of the nature of concepts resulting in their reification. But a weaker version of this argument presents a very serious problem for any comparative research. It is often argued that social events occur in syndromes that have a specific spatiotemporal location; in other words, societies constitute "systems," and therefore various elements of societies interact with each other. Comparisons that disregard syndromes or interaction are based on an assumption that the phenomena to which the same name has been applied are in some way "the same." This assumption will usually be false. The problem, therefore, is to find a set of criteria that can be used to evaluate the appropriateness of comparing social phenomena observed in different social systems. As Osgood has stated:

". . .an interpretation strategy is required to solve such vexing questions as the following: When is the same really the same? When is the same really different? When is different really the same? When is different really different?"[13]

These questions express a common concern in comparative analysis.[14] It seems clear, however, that these problems cannot be solved as long as the metalanguage of comparative analysis is formulated in the language of "comparability," "sameness," "similarity," etc. It will be shown that once the nature of problems involved in cross-national observation are realized, such a metalanguage becomes available and a set of empirical criteria can be applied.

What does it mean that phenomena observed in different social systems are or are not "comparable"? This judgment concerns the possibility of expressing social phenomena in terms of a standard language or, simply, of *measuring* them. Measurement is an operation in which an ordered language is applied to the expression of empirical observations. The criteria required in this operation are explicit: the language must be isomorphic to the phenomena and must represent them in a unique and meaningful way.[15] The degree to which any measuring operation corresponds to these requirements is to some extent represented in terms of criteria of reliability and validity. The reliability criterion tells us to what extent the categories applied to the expression of cross-systemic observations constitute "universals" or are "invariant."[16] Validity tells us to what extent the instrument actually measures what was intended to be measured, that is, to what extent it portrays the observed phenomena as they occur in each social system. Thus the language of measurement theory can be applied as a metalanguage to the problems of cross-national "comparability." The problem whether concepts such as "integration," "urbanization," "market," or "insult" are too general to take into account system-specific variations is a question of ascertaining the validity and reliability of the standard language in which these phenomena are expressed.

[13] C. E. Osgood, "On the Strategy of Cross-National Research into Subjective Culture," *Social Science Information*, **6**, 1967, p. 7.

[14] A particularly interesting discussion of problems of comparability can be found in N. J. Smelser, *op. cit.*

[15] Patrick Suppes and J. L. Zinnes, "Basic Measurement Theory," in R. D. Luce, R. R. Bush and E. Galanter, eds., *Handbook of Mathematical Psychology*, John Wiley & Sons, New York, 1963.

[16] For the concepts of "universality" and "invariance" see Gideon Sjoberg, "The Comparative Method in the Social Sciences," *Philosophy of Science*, **22**, 1955.

Summary and Conclusions

So far we have discussed the assumptions of research that underlie the models of inquiry used in comparative studies. We have attempted to show that some of the disagreements about the possibilities and prospects of cross-societal theories are based on misunderstandings concerning the level of discourse, and some are based on differences of expectations concerning the structure of social reality. We have indicated that the differences between the "relativist" and the "generalist" approaches to social sciences are not insurmountable and can be bridged when their respective assumptions are made explicit. We have concluded that general theory consisting of nomothetic statements can be formulated and tested in the social sciences if proper names of social systems are replaced by variables in the course of comparative research and that most problems of "uniqueness versus universality" can be redefined as problems of measurement. Although we have in general accepted the postulates of the model of inquiry derived from the natural sciences, we have also emphasized the problems involved in the application of this model to social reality.

Social reality may be infinitely diverse. This belief leads some to conclude that social reality can be "understood" only within the context in which it is observed, and can never be explained by general lawlike statements. But those who accept the model of science calling for general statements believe that, regardless of the extent of social diversity, it nonetheless can be expressed in terms of general theories.

In our view the formulation of general theories is possible if and only if these theories take into account what appears to us to be a pervasive property of social reality: social phenomena are not only diverse but always occur in mutually interdependent and interacting structures, possessing a spatiotemporal location. If stable, these patterns of interaction can be treated as systems. Social systems are composed of interacting elements, such as individuals, groups, communities, institutions, or governments. What is important for comparative inquiry is that systems with which we ordinarily deal, such as societies, nations, and cultures, are organized in terms of several levels of components and that the interactions within these systems are not limited to any particular level but cut across these levels. Thus the behavior of any element, such as an individual, depends not only upon his interaction with other individuals but also upon his interaction with institutions such as the church or the state.

If social phenomena are treated as components of systems, two major implications follow. The first is that the behavior of any component of a system is determined by factors intrinsic to the system and is relatively isolated from influences outside of the system. The fact that behavior takes place within a relatively isolated context may mean that a certain proportion of the explanation of this behavior may be found among factors extrinsic to all systems—universal factors—and a certain proportion may be found among factors that are intrinsic to particular systems and not generalizable across systems. Frustration may be a common factor explaining student unrest in all systems; but in addition characteristics of particular systems, such as the structure of Columbia University, may also form a part of the explanation. Our position is that the characteristics of particular systems can be expressed as general variables, such as the presence or absence of student participation in university decision-making, and as such would be applicable across all systems. In fact, whenever there is a system specific factor that seems to be necessary for explanation, the conclusion should not be that systems are unique but rather that it is necessary to identify some general factors so far not considered. This is indeed the primary function of comparative inquiry.

The second implication of treating social phenomena as components of systems is that specific observations must be interpreted within the context of specific systems. Phenomena become facts when they are expressed in some language. The problem is that the same language may not be applicable across all systems but may have to be adjusted to specific systems. This is the central problem of comparative measurement: to incorporate into measurement statements the context within which observations are made. We believe that the existing language of measurement is sufficient to permit contextual adjustments in measurement statements.

These, then, are the major problems in comparative inquiry: to introduce systemic factors into general, theoretical statements and to retain the systemic context of measurement statements. The logical and methodological strategies for solving these problems constitute the subject of this book. Part One deals with problems of theory and Part Two with problems of measurement.

Theory

CHAPTER ONE

Comparative Research and Social Science Theory

*Explanation and Theory in Social Science. Theory and Spatiotemporal
Parameters: The Postulate of Substitutability. The Status of Proper
Names of Systems. Summary.*

While a precise definition of comparative research will not be presented
immediately, we assume in this book that the goal of social science is to
explain social phenomena. We further postulate that the generality and
parsimony of theories should be given primacy over their accuracy. In
other words social science theories, rather than explaining phenomena as
accurately as possible in terms relative to specific historical circumstances,
should attempt to explain phenomena wherever and whenever they occur.
Although this position is not new, this chapter is written with the belief
that the implications of this preference for the conduct of comparative
research will become clear when the assumptions underlying this choice are
understood. We shall first discuss the assumptions underlying the construction of general and parsimonious theories and, second, recommend some
procedures of data-gathering and data analysis in comparative research.
We will argue that the bridge between historically anchored observations
and theoretical statements can be found in comparative studies and that
general theories cannot be constructed in the social sciences without explicit
reference to factors operating at the level of systems.

Explanation and Theory in the Social Sciences

In 1954 in Bennington, Vermont, small businessmen supported the
radical right more often than salaried employees with the same education.
In 1963 in Poland, women who had had premarital sexual experience perceived their marriages as more successful than those who had had no pre-

marital experiences. In 1958 in Finland, persons with congruent status (corresponding levels of income, education, and occupation) voted for the leftist parties more often than persons with incongruent status.

These deliberately selected and disparate findings of social scientists can one day find their way into history books and become a part of the human heritage in such documents as the book relating the eating habits of Frenchmen during the second half of the eighteenth century or some future work reporting on the daily life in Vermont in the middle of the twentieth century. The way in which these findings are formulated makes us think of the future historian: most social scientists are more interested in finding out *why* social phenomena occur than where and when. But all observations of the sociopolitical realm are anchored in time and space. It is in Vermont, Poland, and Finland that these observations are made. They are made at a certain time and in a certain place, and if we were more concerned with historical veracity than with theoretical generality, we would never extend the findings beyond the particular spatiotemporal parameters within which the observations were made. The concern with building general theories of human behavior constitutes such an overriding goal of social scientists, however, that they are willing to risk the error of false generalizations rather than give up that concern.[1] Thus we learn that "frustration brings aggression," that "outgroup hostility breeds ingroup solidarity," that "the disparity of culturally legitimate goals and means results in anomie," and that "a high level of economic development is necessary for a stable democratic political system."

The goal of science is to explain and predict why certain events occur when and where they do. Why did small businessmen in Vermont support McCarthy in 1954? Why was the Kowalski marriage not successful? Why did Smith commit a crime? Why did Napoleon attack Russia? Science is concerned with the explanation of specific events by means of statements that are invariantly true from one set of circumstances to another. But what does it mean to "explain" or "predict" a concrete, specific event?

Since a discussion of "explanation" exceeds the limits of this work, we

[1] A discussion of the types of historical generalizations and errors associated with those generalizations can be found in Stephan Nowak, "General Laws and Historical Generalizations in the Social Sciences," *Polish Sociological Bulletin*, 1, 1961, pp. 21–30. Nowak defines the problem in the following way: "If . . . the sociologist is cautious, he is also alert to the fact that the more the limits of the validity of his theory exceed the investigated reality, the greater is the danger of his statements being false. . . If in addition he [the sociologist] is acquainted with the postulates of the methodology of science, he usually wants his propositions to be universal, free from limitations of time and space, so that they become scientific laws, since he is aware that statements of this type have many particularly valuable theoretical properties."

shall base the subsequent analysis on the paradigm of explanation proposed by C. G. Hempel.[2] Even Hempel's views, however, will not be presented here in their entirety, but will only be used as the basis for the discussion of comparative explanations of social phenomena.

To explain a specific event is to state the conditions under which it always or usually takes place, that is, to cite general statements (laws) from which other statements concerning properties of specific events can be inferred with some reasonable certainty. In the social sciences such an explanation will most often be of a statistical nature. In order to understand why an individual behaved in a certain way in a given situation, we invoke general probabilistic statements that say that, for an individual of a particular type, it is likely that he will behave in this way, given this type of a situation.

For example, why does Monsieur Rouget, age 24, blond hair, brown eyes, a worker in a large factory, vote Communist? To explain the vote of M. Rouget, one must rely upon general probabilistic statements that are relevant for voting behavior and have been sufficiently confirmed against various sets of evidence. The particular features of M. Rouget must be used as the first premise of the explanation:

M. Rouget is a worker and
works in a large factory and
is young (24 years old).

The second premise consists of a conjunction of general statements describing with a high likelihood the behavior of skilled workers, employees of large factories, and young persons. (No interaction is assumed.)

One out of every two workers votes Communist; and employees of large organizations vote Communist more often than employees of small organizations; and young people vote Communist more often than older people.

Therefore, it is likely that
M. Rouget votes Communist.

This explanation is incomplete. The probability of a French worker, 24, employed in a large factory, and voting Communist is still far from 1.00. Several other factors, such as place of residence, marital status, father's occupation, religiosity, and so forth, might have to be considered if the explanation (prediction) of M. Rouget's behavior were to approach certainty. Most explanations in the social sciences are incomplete in the

[2] C. G. Hempel, *Aspects of Scientific Explanation and Other Essays in the Philosophy of Science,* Free Press, New York, 1965. See particularly the title essay, pp. 229–497

sense that the probability of the explained phenomenon taking place does not approach 1.00 (or zero). Since the rules of inference are probabilistic, we cannot expect that, even if the premises are true, the conclusions will invariably follow. As the probability of inferential rules increases, however, the probability of predicting a property also increases—it moves away from what could be expected randomly.

The general statements that serve as premises in an explanation constitute a theory. Usually more than one general statement is necessary to provide a relatively complete explanation. These statements must have certain logical properties: they must be interconnected, and none of their implications can contradict any other implication. Some rules must also be available to determine whether a specific event is an element of the class covered by the theory. In other words, these statements must be empirically interpretable. Finally, the set of such general statements should include a formal deductive framework, such that the inferred consequence is not an intuitively obvious result of the premises. The logical structure of theories, however, is not our central concern.

The accumulation of knowledge consists of the process of gradual confirmation and/or modification of the theories that serve as the general premises in the explanatory scheme. If we are to understand "what happened in the last election in Denmark," "why was there a drop in suicides in Southern Italy," or "what made Joe drop out of school," we must have available a set of general theories sufficiently confirmed to provide a reasonable certainty that when these general statements are applicable, the expected consequences will follow.

At any stage in the development of science it is likely, however, that more than one theory will explain the same class of events. Therefore additional goals are postulated that provide criteria for the evaluation of theories: accuracy, generality, parsimony, and causality.

First, we expect a theory to be accurate, to explain as completely as possible, and to predict as much of the variation as possible. This criterion can be expressed in terms of the amount of variance accounted for by the independent variables—the more variance accounted for by a theory, the smaller the error of prediction. For comparative research this criterion implies that the goal of social science theory is to explain a given phenomenon as accurately as possible *in each social system*. If we wanted to explain the incidence of divorce, for example, we would construct theories that would minimize the error of prediction in each social system. We might find that in one society 99.9 percent of the variance of divorces can be explained by the education of spouses, their religion, and the degree of rigidity. In another social system, we may again be able to account for 99.9 percent of the variance of divorces, but with the use of different factors, for example, mutual perceptions of the spouses, extent of premarital sexual experience, and sexual satisfaction in marriage. The two theories will be maximally accurate. They will provide a nearly complete explanation of divorce in each society. But they will not meet other requirements imposed on theories: accuracy, generality, parsimony, and causality.

When the accuracy of theories is maximized, their generality and parsimony will often be low. Generality of a theory refers to the range of social phenomena to which it is applicable. The greater the generality of a theory, the greater the range of phenomena that can be explained by the theory. For example, one theoretical proposition may state that "education is related to political participation." This theory provides an explanation of one type of political activity of individuals, but only one type of activity. But what are we saying when we identify education as a determinant of behavior? What is "education"? Is it the number of questions concerning different branches of knowledge one is able to answer? The duration of protection of an individual by his family or by society? Reinforcement of certain behavioral patterns by appropriate rewards? Chemical changes in the composition of brain cells? A number of more general theories can be formulated if any of these definitions replaces the definition of education in terms of number of school years completed. For example, a more general theory may state that individuals who have been protected by society over an extended period of time are more likely to participate in social activities. Since attending school usually provides such protection and since political participation is a type of social activity, the original, less general theory can be deduced from the more general one. The development of natural science consists of more general theories superseding less general theories. As Hempel points out:

"When a scientific theory is superseded by another in the sense in which classical mechanics and electrodynamics were superseded by the special theory of relativity, then the succeeding theory will generally have a wider explanatory range, including phenomena the earlier theory could not account for; and it will as a rule provide approximative explanations for the empirical laws implied by its predecessor."[3]

In social science, however, it is not always apparent that a less general theory can be deduced from a more general theory even if both are avail-

[3] *Ibid.*, p. 345.

able. Both reward theory and a theory of political participation may potentially explain why an individual votes in an election; but it is not apparent that the explanatory role of education can be deduced from the reward theory or any other psychological theory.

In the example discussed above, 99.9 percent of variance of divorce is predicted in each social system, but not a single statement can be made that would be true for both systems. Such an explanation will not only lack generality but also will not be parsimonious. The smaller the number of factors providing for a complete explanation of a given class of events, the more parsimonious the theory.[4] It would be an interesting experiment to compare the interpretations given to findings derived from particular countries with the interpretations of similar data from various countries. Why were third parties never spectacularly successful in the United States? Because of the bipartisan tradition. Why were third parties never successful in Great Britain? Because of the shift in the composition of the labor force that took the working-class support away from the Liberals and gave it to Labour. But when we confront the two questions simultaneously—why were third parties never particularly successful in either country—the answer will tend to be formulated in terms of factors common to both such as the electoral system. To the extent that different theories—each involving a different set of independent variables—are used for different social systems, the formulation and testing of general theories in the social sciences is not possible.

The criteria of generality and parsimony imply that the same theories must be evaluated in different systemic settings and that social science theories can gain confirmation only if theories formulated in terms of the common factors constitute the point of departure for comparative research. We recognize, however, that in some situations accuracy in a particular social system may be the most important value. For example, if we want to predict election results in the United States, we probably will not be concerned with the same factors that will predict election results in Great Britain. But if the goal is to provide understanding as to why people identify with political parties, then generality and parsimony will be more important than system-specific accuracy. If the role of a theory is to provide immediate

---

[4] The number of factors is only one of many aspects of parsimony. For a full discussion of this concept and its many definitions see the summary of the writings of Janina Kotarbinska in Henryk Skolimowski, *Polish Analytical Philosophy*, Routledge, Kegan and Paul, London, 1967.

guidelines for social practice, then accuracy in a specific social system may be the most important value.[5]

The fourth criterion imposed on theory concerns causality. We can think of causality in a twofold perspective. Causality is a property of a system of variables. A system of variables is said to be causal to the extent that (1) the dependent variable is not "overdetermined"—no two variables within the system explain the same part of the variation of the dependent phenomenon and (2) the system of variables is isolated—the explanatory pattern does not change when new variables are added.[6] The extent to which a theory is causal, that is, the extent to which general premises are invariant, increases as the number of factors incorporated into the theory increases. In terms of comparative research, the postulate of causality implies that factors operating at different levels of analysis—groups, communities, region, nations, etc.—should be incorporated into theories and that their interaction with the factors operating within each of these systems should be examined.

This particular model of theory as a general, parsimonious, and causal set of statements is assumed throughout the rest of this book. We are not arguing that this particular model constitutes the only or even the best model of theory, but that if this model is accepted, then cross-systemic studies must become an integral part of theory-building and theory-testing.

[5] As W. E. Moore, has stated, generalization involves abstraction and abstraction involves a loss of information. "No [general] theory will yield a *specific* prediction, or yield a *specific* guide to policy . . . except by reversing the process and adding information to the general proposition." W. E. Moore, "The Social Framework of Economic Development," in R. J. Braibanti and J. J. Spengler, eds., *Tradition, Values, and Socio-Economic Development,* Duke University Press, Durham, N.C., 1961, p. 58.

[6] The first aspect of causality—the problem of overdetermination—has recently become fashionable among social scientists, following Simon's article on "Causal Ordering and Identifiability" in W. C. Hood and T. C. Koopmans, eds., *Studies in Econometric Method,* John Wiley & Sons, New York, 1953. Overdetermination can be tested, if strong assumptions are accepted, through the analysis of partial correlations or partial path coefficients. The second aspect of causality has so far received only lip service. The assumption of uncorrelated errors is usually stated but not tested. It seems that Hempel came closest to suggesting an empirical test of this assumption in postulating the criterion of "maximal specificity" *(op. cit.,* p. 402). This criterion implies that causal explanations should be accepted tentatively and then subjugated to the tests of invariance under the addition of new variables. If and only if the path coefficients do not change substantively when new variables are introduced, the assumption of relative isolation of the system of variables can be maintained.

Theory and Spatiotemporal Parameters:
The Postulate of Substitutability

In the Introduction we defined some general issues underlying the alleged contradiction between historically based observations and abstractly formulated statements. A question often discussed by students of society is whether historically anchored observations should be treated as specific to particular social systems or whether general theories, free of spatiotemporal parameters, can be developed and tested. As indicated earlier, the issue no longer appears in this extreme form. The problem now is to define the conditions under which general theories can be developed and the procedures that are appropriate for the development and testing of general theories.

The extreme version of the relativistic argument allows no way of bridging historical and theoretical statements. Once a proposition is stated in historical terms, using such proper names as Ghana, Hitler, or British workers during the 1950s, it could be incorporated only into a theory consisting of more general historical propositions, containing such names as Africa, German leaders, or the British population during the 1950s. If, however, a proposition is stated in terms free of proper names, it can be incorporated only into theories consisting exclusively of such propositions. For example, the proposition that "economic crises give rise to charismatic leadership" can be generalized into a statement that "all crises give rise to charismatic leadership."

This distinction between historical and theoretical generalization clarifies the alternative modes of theory construction. Any set of observations can be generalized in one of two ways, depending upon whether historical or theoretical generality is sought. But this distinction is only analytical. Actually spatiotemporal propositions (e.g., measurement statements) can be generalized theoretically, and general statements can be specified historically. On the one hand, the statement that "Hitler was a charismatic leader who came to power in Germany as a result of a crisis" can be generalized into a theoretical proposition relating crises and charismatic leadership. On the other hand, the statement that "crises give rise to charismatic leaders" may have been observed to be true only in Africa. Thus the observed historical situation is not unique, but neither is the general theoretical statement universal. Historical statements are implicitly theoretical. They subsume under the proper names of the social systems a broad range of factors that might be used in theoretical explanation. But theoretical statements will generally include a historical component. As long as Africa differs from the other parts of the world, theoretical analysis is no longer possible, and therefore the name of a social system will have to be used in explanation. Thus "unique" factors can neither be the only ones nor can they be totally discarded in theoretical analysis. They are redefined, rather, as the residuum of theoretical explanation.

The bridge between historical observations and general theory is the substitution of variables for proper names of social systems in the course of comparative research. The theoretical importance of this statement is best understood in terms of Hempel's requirement that classes of events referred to in theoretical ("lawlike") statements be essentially generalizable. Hempel argued:

"Surely a lawlike sentence must not be *logically* limited to a finite number of instances: it must not be logically equivalent to a finite conjunction of singular sentences, or, briefly, it must be of essentially generalized form."[7]

For example, a statement that "all Mexicans are taller than all Americans" is not a lawlike sentence that can be used for the explanation of the height of Mexicans or Americans. This sentence is logically equivalent to a conjunction of statements giving all asymmetrical relations between individual Mexicans and Americans, and it cannot sustain counterfactual and subjunctive conditional statements such as "if Mr. X, who is an American were a Mexican, he would have been taller." The sentence, "Persons living in warmer climates are invariably taller than persons living in colder climates," however, is not a conjunction of any finite number of statements concerning individuals; it can, at least logically, be extended ad infinitum. In other words, *lawlike statements are possible in the social sciences if and only if spatiotemporal parameters are treated as residua of variables potentially contributing to the explanation.*

The postulate of substitutability concerns the ontological status of such concepts as "group," "organization," "culture," "nation," and "political system"—the ontological status of systems enclosed within some specific spatial and temporal parameters. Before proceeding to the discussion of this postulate and its implications, we will analyze more closely the notion of "historically located social systems," or "spatiotemporal parameters."

A concept of "all historical social systems" or "all spatiotemporal parameters" obviously defines the maximal levels of generality for any statement. Nothing can be more general than always and everywhere. This concept defines the entire population of conditions within which observations of social phenomena can be made, and any particular set of observations is a sample, random or not, of this population. We can conceive of the set of historical circumstances of the most general nature that contains all historical social systems or spatiotemporal parameters. This set becomes denumerable if additional assumptions are made.

[7] Hempel, *op. cit.,* p. 340.

One such assumption is that this set contains "systems relatively isolated by some factor."[8] For example, human beings allegedly shared some characteristics not shared by animals. Some historical fact, whether it was the elevation to the biped or the acquisition of the superego, defined the "relatively isolated system"—human beings. This type of isolated system of humans is often assumed by psychologists without regard for other isolating factors. Systems can be isolated on the bases of all kinds of historical events that determined any one of their common characteristics. Classifications of civilizations provide an example of systems isolated with regard to some basic cultural influence, such as "Judeo-Christian," "Sanskrit," and "Incan." Any denumeration in terms of relatively isolated systems is, obviously, a hypothetical one. Cross-system research must demonstrate that differences within those systems are indeed smaller than the differences among them.

Another way denumerating the set of all spatiotemporal parameters consists of finding some cutoff point in the past, such as a listing of countries that existed after World War II. This set is first defined temporally and then denumerated in terms of countries or "nations." In the light of this discussion of "relatively isolated systems," it is clear that there are many ways of denumerating the set of all historical circumstances. The alternatives range from denumerating it as a set consisting of one element, "the animal," to denumeration in terms of any observable subsystem. If we limit the temporal parameters and confine the spatial dimension to nations, we would be able to enumerate those systems that constitute the universe in cross-national research. The problem of "uniqueness versus generality" in cross-national studies concerns, therefore, the ontological status of such proper names as Mexico, Ghana, Australia, or Yugoslavia.

The Status of Proper Names of Systems

In Germany and Sweden, better-paid workers are likely to be class conscious, whereas in Britain, the United States, and Australia, the less well-paid workers are class conscious.[9] How can we interpret this finding?

In one interpretation this finding is a "historical generalization," since it specifies the spatiotemporal parameters and encloses the statement about relationships within those parameters. In another interpretation, this finding is a "general proposition" stating that the relationship between income of workers and the extent of their class-consciousness depends upon some

[8] The notion of "relatively isolated systems" was introduced by S. Ossowski, "Two Conceptions of Historical Generalizations," *The Polish Sociological Bulletin*, **9**, 1964.
[9] Reinhard Bendix and S. M. Lipset, "The Field of Political Sociology," in L. A. Coser, ed., *Political Sociology*, Harper and Row, New York, 1966, p. 32.

other factors not yet considered. The nature of the countries might at the most provide a clue as to what these factors might be.

Consider the example of the relationship between motivation to learn a foreign language and grades among the students of various departments at the same university. In some departments such a relationship can be observed; in others it cannot. Should the interpretation of this finding be that "at the University of Warsaw during the 1960s, there is a relationship between motivation and grades in the English department, but not in the French department" or that "the relationship between motivation and grades depends upon the department of the university"?

It should be noted that in both examples we are dealing with situations that are ostensibly experimental. A relationship is being examined separately in two groups of subjects, random samples of populations of countries or university departments. Formally, the situation seems to be analogous to an experiment examining the relationship between motivation and grades in two groups taught by different methods. There are two groups within which two variables are assessed for each individual and for which a numerical value of the relationship can be established. In the experimental situation, however, the individuals are randomly drawn into groups from a single population, and it can be assumed that the error (the influence of other factors, such as intelligence) is not correlated with group membership.

The situation faced in comparative research is not experimental. Specific spatiotemporal parameters, or names of systems, are not equivalent to experimental variables, such as method of instruction. Indeed, we do not know what the experimental variables are. Furthermore, in an experimental situation it is possible to ask what would be a person's value on the dependent variable if he belonged to a different group. This question is justified on the assumption that membership in a group is randomly determined. Consequently if a person were taught by a different method, his performance would have been different. Whether this question and, in general, the use of "controlling and correcting" techniques are equally legitimate in cross-national situations is not clear. If spatiotemporal parameters are understood historically—as not reducible to variables—conditional statements such as "if a person belonging to group (country) *A*, belonged to group (country) *B*, then . . ." or "if group *A* had the same amount of trait . . . as group *B*, then . . ." are clearly unjustifiable. This problem can be illustrated with an example derived from *The Civic Culture*.[10]

[10] G. A. Almond and Sidney Verba, *The Civic Culture,* Princeton University Press, Princeton, N.J., 1963, p. 122. We have discussed this example in our earlier article, "Equivalence in Cross-National Research," *Public Opinion Quarterly,* **30**, 1966–67, admittedly without awareness of the assumptions underlying our recommendation.

Almond and Verba present the following table which relates education and the "feeling of freedom to discuss politics" in five countries.

Table 1   Feeling of Relative Freedom to Discuss Politics, by National and Education [a]

		Education						
	Total		Primary or Less		Some Secondary		Some University	
Nation	%	(N)	%	(N)	%	(N)	%	(N)
United States	63	(969)	49	(338)	70	(443)	71	(188)
Great Britain	63	(939)	59	(593)	70	(322)	83	(24)
Germany	38	(940)	35	(790)	52	(124)	60	(26)
Italy	37	(991)	30	(692)	53	(245)	59	(54)
Mexico	41	(1004)	39	(877)	54	(103)	54	(24)

[a] Numbers in parentheses refer to the bases upon which percentages are calculated.

One historical and one theoretical statement can be derived from these data: (1) The intensity of the feeling of freedom to discuss politics is highest in Britain and the United States, lower in Mexico, and so forth. (2) Education is positively related to the feeling of freedom to discuss politics.

Interpreting these data theoretically, we can ask what the intensity of the feeling of freedom to discuss politics *would have been* if the level of education were the same in all five countries. The grouping of individuals into countries is not random. Indeed, for each individual the probability of inclusion is 1.00 for one country and 0.00 for all other countries. Nonetheless, the influence of education can be randomized ex post facto by some statistical techniques. If the names of the countries are replaced by a variable (in this case level of education), the originally observed differences among countires can be modified to take this factor into account. The resulting statements will still be historical: they will compare countries identified by names. But at least one component of the proper names of these countries has been replaced by a variable free from historical specification.

In order to provide an illustration, education will be treated as if it were expressed on an interval scale. ("Some university education" is scored as 3, "some secondary education" as 2, and "primary or less" as 1.) The average educational level in each country can now be calculated. When the regression of "freedom to discuss politics" on education is analyzed and the means of "freedom to discuss" are accordingly adjusted, the original values undergo a substantial change.

Table 2   Original and Adjusted Means of Relative Freedom to Discuss
Politics, by Nation and Education

Nation	Freedom (Original)	Education	Adjustment .345 $(x_i - x)$	Freedom (Adjusted)
United States	.63	1.84	.1578	.47
Great Britain	.63	1.39	.0034	.63
Germany	.38	1.19	−.0655	.45
Italy	.37	1.36	−.0069	.38
Mexico	.41	1.11	−.0931	.50

After adjusting for the level of education, Great Britain is clearly first with regard to "freedom to discuss politics," Mexico is second, and the United States is third. One theoretical proposition and one including both a theoretical and a historical component can now be formulated: (1) Education is related to freedom to discuss politics. (2) If the educational level in these countries (names) *would have been* the same, *then. . . ."*

Since Mexico is Mexico and the United States is the United States, many will consider statement No. 2 to be nonsensical. As has been discussed, one of the main problems in generalizing across spatiotemporal parameters stems from the fact that social phenomena are either "functionally interdependent" or "interrelated in syndromes" that have specific historical localizations. Therefore a change of one element of these syndromes would bring about not only a change in the other elements, but a change in the entire pattern. For a fully developed theory, however, this change may not be much of a problem since an entire set of interconnected phenomena can be handled at the same time.

The basic assumption is that names of nations, or of social systems in general, are treated as residua of variables that influence the phenomenon being explained but have not yet been considered. Thus such concepts as "culture," "nation," "society," and "political system," are treated as residua of variables, which can be incorporated into a general theory. If the statements reporting particular observations without specifying the spatiotemporal parameters are elliptical, then statements of a historical nature are also elliptical if they do not list the variables that are implicit under the specification of the historical conditions. The often emphasized historical ellipticalness of theoretical statements has its direct counterpart in the theoretical ellipticalness of historical statements.

If we accept this residual nature of names of social systems, we can then attempt to replace these names by variables. When we find that societies differ with regard to a particular characteristic, we can ask what it is about these societies that causes this difference. If the factor first considered does not answer this question satisfactorily, it is possible to consider other factors, gradually replacing the notion that "nations differ" by statements formulated in terms of specific variables. Instead of stating differences among countries with regard to perceived freedom to discuss politics, we may thus formulate a statement that explains freedom to discuss politics in terms of education, perceived distance among parties, and extent of exposure to mass media.

Can the entire content of system residua be exhausted? The answer in principle is positive. Since the number of societies, cultures of political systems is highly limited and the number of relevant variables is very high, however, we may often find that explanatory systems will be overdetermined. The number of observations or degrees of freedom will be too small to allow consideration of all relevant factors. This disparity between the model and the practice of science will result in statements that will generally have a historical residuum—statements in which names of social systems will be cited after theoretical explanations have been exhausted. Although "specific" factors may not be completely removed, they are reinterpreted as residua from theoretical explanation.

Summary

The role of social science is to explain social events. Explanation consists of applying general sentences or, more precisely, theories or sets of such general sentences, to particular events. If the explanation is to be general, parsimonious, and causal, then the accumulation of knowledge—confirmation and/or modification of theories—must involve comparative research. However, explanation in comparative research is possible if and only if particular social systems observed in time and space are not viewed as finite conjunctions of constituent elements, but rather as residua of theoretical variables. General lawlike sentences can be utilized for explanatory purposes. Only if the classes of social events are viewed as generalizable beyond the limits of any particular historical social system can general lawlike sentences be used for explanation. Therefore the role of comparative research in the process of theory-building and theory-testing consists of replacing proper names of social systems by the relevant variables.

CHAPTER TWO

Research Designs

"Most Similar Systems" Designs. "Most Different Systems" Designs.
Univariate Comparisons. Comparing Relationships.

Most comparative studies take as their point of departure the known differences among social systems and examine the impact of these differences on some other social phenomena observed within these systems. An alternative strategy, however, is available. With this strategy, differences among systems are taken into account as they are encountered in the process of explaining social phenomena observed within these systems. Although emphasis will be placed on the latter strategy, the assumptions and implications of both strategies will be the subject of this chapter.

As discussed in the previous chapter, a general theory is composed of propositions formulated in terms of variables observed either within social systems or at the level of systems, but devoid of the names of social systems. Since the number of the relevant determinants of any kind of social behavior is likely to exceed the number of accessible social systems, the objective of a theory free of all proper names will not be easily reached, and thus procedures must be formulated to maximize this objective.

All research involves defining the population for which the study is to be conducted and selecting a sample from this population. Sampling methods vary greatly, depending upon the problems of the research and the nature of the population. Sometimes the sample is a random selection from the entire universe; sometimes it is selected in several steps in which some larger social units are chosen first and other social units within them are sampled subsequently; in other cases the sample is "stratified"—individuals are selected on the basis of their position on some variable, such as income or education. The common and obvious procedure in cross-systemic re-

31

search is to first select systems and then to sample individuals or groups within them.

For practical reasons the selection of countries can rarely be random. Even though the universe of social systems—countries, nation-states, cultures, and so forth—is fairly limited, the costs of conducting a study within random samples taken within each system will for a long time remain prohibitive. Therefore cross-national studies often have a quasi-experimental form, and the tactical choices are limited to the question of the "best" combination of countries, given the overwhelming limitations of money, access, and social scientists.

"Most Similar Systems" Design

The currently predominant view among social scientists seems to opt for the strategy that Naroll calls studies of "concomitant variation."[1] Such studies are based on the belief that systems as similar as possible with respect to as many features as possible constitute the optimal samples for comparative inquiry. For example, Scandinavian countries or the two-party systems of the Anglo-Saxon countries are seen as good samples because these countries share many economic, cultural, and political characteristics; therefore the number of "experimental" variables, although unknown and still large, is minimized. This type of design is a "maximim" strategy. It is anticipated that if some important differences are found among these otherwise similar countries, then the number of factors attributable to these differences will be sufficiently small to warrant explanation in terms of those differences alone. A difference in the intensity of political partisanship between Sweden and Finland can be attributed to a smaller number of intersystem differences than between Sweden and Japan.

Alford's study of social determinants of voting was based on this kind of perspective. Describing the choice of countries, Alford noted:

"The Anglo-American countries—Great Britain, Australia, New Zealand, the United States, and Canada—are alike in the important respect that they may be termed "pluralist" political systems. . . . Each of the Anglo-American countries tends toward a two-party system. . . . The electorate is not fragmented into supporters of one or another small party hoping to gain a few seats and a voice in a coalition government."[2]

[1] Raoul Naroll, "Some Thoughts on Comparative Method in Cultural Anthropology," in H. M. Blalock and Ann Blalock, eds. *Methodology in Social Research,* McGraw-Hill, New York, 1968.

[2] R. R. Alford, "Party and Society," in F. J. Munger, ed., *Studies in Comparative Politics,* Thomas Crowell, New York, 1967, pp. 66–67.

He then discussed the differences between this set of countries and the multi-party systems of continental Europe, such as the relatively minor importance of religion as a determinant of voting among the Anglo-American countries. Finally, Alford specified the factors that differentiate the Anglo-American countries and that might explain the differences in the extent of class-voting. Allardt considered in similar terms the differences in class-voting among the Scandinavian countries and attributed the relatively high extent of such voting in Finland to the comparatively lower mobility rates in that country.[3] In their study of civic culture Almond and Verba chose countries that have a "democratic political system" but differ with regard to their level of development.[4] Studies of social mobility[5] and suicide[6] in Scandinavia followed this strategy. Cantril's[7] and Dogan's[8] studies of Communist voting in France and Italy took as their point of departure the similarities between these political systems. This is also the perspective of the "area study" approaches in the social sciences, whether the area is defined in cultural or political terms.

Intersystemic similarities and intersystemic differences are the focus of the "most similar systems" designs. Systems constitute the original level of analysis, and within-system variations are explained in terms of systemic factors. Although these designs rarely have been formulated rigorously, their logic is fairly clear. Common systemic characteristics are conceived of as "controlled for," whereas intersystemic differences are viewed as explanatory variables. The number of common characteristics sought is maximal and the number of not shared characteristics sought, minimal. The resulting statements will take the following form: "Among the Anglo-American countries, which share the following characteristics. . . , differences with regard to class voting can be attributed to the following factors. . . ." There is no reason why these statements have to be formulated exclusively at the systemic level. One might find, for example, that among democratic countries that are economically developed, church at-

[3] Erik Allardt, "Patterns of Class Conflict and Working Class Consciousness in Finnish Politics," Publications of the Institute of Sociology, University of Helsinki, No. 30, 1964.

[4] G. A. Almond and Sidney Verba, *The Civic Culture*, Princeton University Press, Princeton, N.J., 1963.

[5] Kaare Svalastoga, *Prestige, Class, and Mobility*, Gyldenal Scandinavian University Books, Copenhagen, 1959.

[6] Habat Hendin, *Suicide in Scandinavia: A Psychoanalytic Study of Culture and Character*, Grune & Stratton, New York, 1964.

[7] Hadley Cantril, *The Politics of Despair*, Basic Books, New York, 1958.

[8] Mattei Dogan, "Political Cleavage and Social Stratification in France and Italy," in S. M. Lipset and Stein Rokkan, eds., *Party Systems and Voter Alignments: Cross-National Perspectives*, Free Press, New York, 1967.

tendance is either positively or not at all related to party identification, whereas among the less-developed democratic countries the relationship is negative.[9]

If such a difference is found among the systems studied, the following theoretical implications follow: (1) The factors that are common to the countries are irrelevant in determining the behavior being explained since different patterns of behavior are observed among systems sharing these factors. (2) Any set of variables that differentiates these systems in a manner corresponding to the observed differences of behavior (or any interaction among these differences) can be considered as explaining these patterns of behavior. The second implication is particularly important. Although the number of differences among similar countries is limited, it will almost invariably be sufficiently large to "overdetermine" the dependent phenomenon. Although "most similar systems" designs focus on concomitant variation, the experimental variables cannot be singled out. There is more than one factor that ranks Great Britain, Australia, the United States, and Canada in the same order; there is more than one difference between the United States, Great Britain, and West Germany, on the one hand, and Italy and Mexico on the other. But even if we assume that some differences can be identified as determinants, the efficiency of this strategy in providing knowledge that can be generalized is relatively limited.

"Most Different Systems" Design

The alternative strategy takes as the starting point the variation of the observed behavior at a level lower than that of systems. Most often this will be the level of individual actors, but it can be the level of groups, local communities, social classes, or occupations. Although the goal of this strategy is the same as in the "similar systems" design, systemic factors are not given any special place among the possible predictors of behavior. For example, we may be interested in explaining variations in college student attitudes toward personal adjustment,[10] perceptional illusion of movement,[11] values of youth,[12] or values of local leaders.[13] The initial assumption is that

[9] G. A. Almond and Sidney Verba, *op. cit.*

[10] J. M. Gillespie and G. W. Allport, *Youth's Outlook on the Future: A Cross-National Study,* Doubleday, New York, 1955.

[11] G. W. Allport and Thomas Pettigrew, "Cultural Influence on the Perception of Movement: The Trapezoidal Illusion among Zulus," *Journal of Abnormal and Social Psychology,* **55**, 1957.

[12] H. H. Hyman, Arif Payaslioglu, and F. W. Frey, "The Values of Turkish College Youth," *Public Opinion Quarterly,* **22**, 1958.

[13] P. E. Jacob, Henry Teune, and T. M. Watts, "Values, Leadership, and Development," *Social Science Information,* **7**, 1968.

individuals were drawn from the same population; in other words, that systemic factors do not play any role in explaining the observed behavior. Further investigation consists of testing, step by step, this assumption in the course of cross-systemic research. As long as this assumption is not rejected, the analysis remains at the *intrasystemic* level; whenever the assumption is rejected, systemic factors must be considered.

The first step in this design is to identify those independent variables, observed within systems, that do not violate the assumption of the homogeneity of the total population. Although the samples are derived from different systems, they are initially treated as if the population from which they are drawn is homogeneous. If the subgroups of the population derived from different systems do not differ with regard to the dependent variable, the differences among these systems are not important in explaining this variable. If the relationship between an independent and the dependent variable is the same within the subgroups of the population, then again the systemic differences need not be taken into consideration.

To the extent that general statements can be validly formulated without regard to the social systems from which the samples were drawn, systemic factors can be disregarded. If rates of suicide are the same among the Zuni, the Swedes, and the Russians, those factors that distinguish these three societies are irrelevant for the explanation of suicide. If education is positively related to attitudes of internationalism in India, Ireland, and Italy, the differences among these countries are unimportant in explaining internationalist attitudes. Whereas studies of concomitant variation require positive identification of relevant systemic factors, the "most different systems" design centers on eliminating irrelevant systemic factors.

The difference between the two strategies should not be overemphasized. Both strategies can result in the confirmation of theoretical statements and both can combine intrasystemic and intersystemic levels of analysis. In the most different systems design, the level of analysis is shifted to systemic factors when the formulation of valid general statements is no longer possible for all of the subpopulations. If it is found that attitudes of internationalism in India and Iran depend upon exposure to mass media but do not in Ireland and Italy, then the differences between the two sets of systems become relevant and reference must be made to the systemic level. When this is necessary, concomitant variation is studied ex post facto, and intersystemic differences are attributed to the observed variations within systems.

Concomitant variation studies are focused almost exclusively at the level of systems. Certain systemic traits are held constant, and others are allowed to vary. Denumeration in terms of national social or political systems or cultures is only one of the many possible ways of conceptualizing social systems as the units of analysis in any theory. One could design research at the level of the American states, Finnish regions, Peruvian villages, Northern Californian tribes, and so forth. Similar systems designs, however, require an a priori assumption about the level of social systems at which the important factors operate. Once a particular design is formulated, assumptions concerning alternative levels of systems cannot be considered. The original assumption can be tested only in its entirety—either the systemic factors of the specified level of social systems are or are not relevant.

In the most different systems design, the question of at which level the relevant factors operate remains open throughout the process of inquiry. *The point of departure of this design is the population of units at the lowest level observed in the study, most often individuals.* The design calls for testing whether this population is homogeneous. If subgroups of this population that correspond to some identifiable levels of social systems can be distinguished empirically, then factors operating at this level of systems will be considered. If a population of individuals is sampled from several communities within several countries, then differences among individuals will be tested both within and across communities and within and across countries. If communities differ, systemic factors operating at the level of local communities will be considered; if nations differ, national factors will be examined; if neither countries nor communities differ, the entire analysis will remain at the individual level and no systemic factors will be considered. The level that reduces to the greatest extent the within-group variance will be considered.

Although the subsequent technical discussion is based on a multiple regression model, it is also possible to visualize this design as one in which the patterns of interaction are being systematically examined for alternative ways of grouping individuals, whether based on a classification of various levels of social systems or some attributes measured at the individual level.[14] Whenever classification into some level of systems results in the greatest reduction in variance and therefore yields the greatest gain in prediction, the level of analysis is shifted to factors operating at this level.

In the context of this design, the definition of comparative research becomes clear. *Comparative research is inquiry in which more than one level of analysis is possible and the units of observation are identifiable by name*

---

[14] Computer programs that operate in a "tree" fashion and study interaction independently for each "branch" (e.g., the Automatic Interaction Detector) may be most suitable for this purpose.

at each of these levels.[15] Thus a study of local leaders sampled from local communities in a single country is comparative, since research can proceed at both the individual and at the community levels. But if supranational regions are not identifiable, according to this definition a study conducted exclusively at the level of countries is not comparative.

Since the goal of research is to confirm general statements about human behavior, the process of sampling, even if it is not random, should be oriented toward this goal. No research based on a design other than a random multistep sample of all social systems will allow universal generalizations. The validity of generalizations and the guidelines for further research provided by the two research strategies will depend upon the nature of the findings that they respectively bring. Findings desirable in the most similar systems design are highly undesirable in the most different systems design and vice versa. Let us discuss this statement.

In the most similar systems design, systems with as many similar characteristics as possible are sought. Without attempting to provide a list, let the characteristics shared by the Scandinavian countries be denoted as $X_1, X_2, \ldots, X_k$, and the characteristics that are not shared as $X_{k+1}, Y_{k+2}, \ldots, X_n$. A dependent variable, whether it is a frequency distribution of one variable or a relationship between two variables, is found to vary among these highly similar countries. For example, according to Allardt the amount of class voting varies among the Scandinavian countries[16] A data matrix for five countries in this kind of a design would assume the following form (all variables are dichotomized):

Country	Variables Controlled				"Experimental" Variables		Dependent Variable
	X_1	X_2 $\cdots$	$\cdots$	X_k	X_{k+1} $\cdots$	X_n	Y (or $X_s Y_s$)
A	1	1 $\cdots$	$\cdots$	0	1 $\cdots$	1	1
B	1	1 $\cdots$	$\cdots$	0	0 $\cdots$	0	0
C	1	1 $\cdots$	$\cdots$	0	1 $\cdots$	1	1
D	1	1 $\cdots$	$\cdots$	0	1 $\cdots$	1	1
E	1	1 $\cdots$	$\cdots$	0	0 $\cdots$	0	0

The dependent phenomenon can either be a single aggregated attribute or a within-system relationship. Of course there are other factors that differentiate these systems in ways *not* associated with the variations of the dependent variable. The resulting finding, if stated carefully, may take the following form: "When the observed systems share characteristics $X_1, X_2,$

---

[15] It should be noted that this is the meaning of the term "comparative" as used in psychology. Comparative psychology is a study of organisms at different levels of structural differentiation.

[16] Erik Allardt, *op. cit.*

..., X_k, the variations of the dependent variable Y (or of the relationship between an independent variable X_s *and the dependent variable* Y_s, both measured within systems) are associated with the variable X_{k+1} (according to the hypothesis) or the alternative variables $X_{k+2}, \ldots, X_n$ (alternative hypotheses)."

What further implications follow from this finding? We obtain a positive, although overdetermined, explanation of the dependent variable Y—it either depends upon X_{k+1}, as hypothesized, or the variables $X_{k+2}, \ldots, X_n$, which are not controlled. The original hypothesis is confirmed, although alternative hypotheses are not rejected. This certainly strengthens our confidence in the explanatory power of factor X_{k+1}, and, although no rigorous inferences are possible, further research is directed toward testing the influence of X_{k+1} in other settings.[17] Thus if we find some other social system that shares with these systems all of the characteristics, $X_1, \ldots, X_k$, it is likely that a similar explanatory pattern will be found. If, however, any one of these characteristics is different, no inferences are possible since it is likely that this particular trait interacts with the dependent variable.

If a hypothesis is confirmed as a result of the most similar systems design, we gain some encouragement about the generality of the hypothesis. For example, if we find that among Scandinavian countries frequency of social mobility is associated with the frequency of class voting, we will be prompted to test whether mobility is also associated with class voting among the Anglo-Saxon countries. Moreover if we find that among the Anglo-Saxon countries, which share characteristics *other* than those shared by Scandinavian countries, mobility is also associated with class voting, the confidence in the explanatory power of mobility will be further strengthened. If, however, mobility is not related to class voting among the Anglo-Saxon countries, we are back where we started. All we now know is that class voting depends upon mobility, which in turn depends upon other factors that cannot be isolated.

The logic of the most similar systems design is based on the assumption that characteristics shared by one group of systems, such as Scandinavian countries, can be removed one-by-one in quasi-experimental manner. But this is an unrealistic assumption. As we argued previously, social phenomena vary in syndromes and it is difficult to isolate experimental factors.

---

[17] Let us note that we are talking here in psychological and not in logical terms. Within the present logic of inference, one cannot make any generalization beyond the population from which the sample has been drawn. However, it is apparent that such theory of induction is not appropriate for social science and that, in their practical activities, social scientists are actually willing to take the risk of false generalizations rather than satisfy themselves with rigorous inferences about accidental populations.

The most different systems designs eliminate factors differentiating social systems by formulating statements that are valid regardless of the systems within which observations are made. As long as these statements continue to be true in all systems, no reference to systemic characteristics is made. As soon as additional statements cannot be validly formulated across systems, however, the hypothesis concerning no difference among systems has to be rejected and the level of analysis is shifted to systemic factors. At this point, the association of the intersystemic variations with the intra-systemic differences would be examined. For example, if in a group of systems political participation is positively related to education but the remaining differences in political participation cannot be explained by any other variable measured within systems, it would be necessary to identify the systemic factors associated with these differences. It should be em-phasized that the systemic characteristics need not be dichotomous. For example, one may relate the within-system correlations between budgetary requests and budgetary appropriations to characteristics of American states, such as their per capita income or the degree of interparty competition.

Both of these strategies are based on some expectations about social reality. The most similar systems design is based on a belief that a number of theoretically significant differences will be found among similar systems and that these differences can be used in explanation. The alternative design, which seeks maximal heterogeneity in the sample of systems, is based on a belief that in spite of intersystemic differentiation, the populations will differ with regard to only a limited number of variables or relationships. On the one hand, if it turns out that Swedes, Finns, Norwegians, and Danes are alike in all of the examined aspects of their social behavior, then the study of these countries will not permit the identification of the systemic factors relevant for a particular kind of behavior. If, on the other hand, Americans, Indians, Chileans, and Japanese show no common patterns of behavior, a study of these countries will end up with four separate sets of statements contributing equally little to general theory.

Univariate Comparisons

Underlying the preceding discussion is a set of statements concerning the "sameness" of samples derived from different social systems. Systemic factors can be attributed to within-system variables if the systems are found to be "different" either with respect to a single variable, aggregated at the system level, or with regard to within-system relationships. By the same token, systemic factors can be eliminated from explanation if within-system patterns are found to be the "same." Any formulation of a problem of inquiry as comparative is based on the assumption that factors subsumed under the proper names of systems may potentially influence the phenomena that are being explained.

If systemic factors do indeed influence the within-system patterns, whether univariate or multivariate distributions, then identification of the system within which an observation is made raises our ability to predict a score on the dependent variable above the prediction based only on the mean score for the entire, or "total" population. The coefficient of regression of an individual's score on a variable representing his membership in a particular system must be larger than zero if the population is heterogeneous in terms of systems.

As an example, suppose we are examining individual propensity to vote for the parties of the right among Western European countries. If the proportion of the electorate voting for the parties of the right is the same in all countries, it becomes quite irrelevant whether an individual is a Frenchman or an Italian. Other factors are important, for example, social class or religion. If the members of the Western European elites share similar attitudes toward European integration, again it is not important whether a particular person is a member of the Dutch or the Italian elite. To the extent that identifying the social system does not help predict individual characteristics, systematic factors are not important. The total population is homogeneous, and further research is not distinct from investigations customarily conducted within a single social system. The analysis can proceed at the level of individual characteristics without resorting to any system-level variables.

If it can be assumed that the measurement of a given variable is relatively free of systematic error at the system level and if the scale of measurement is known, a simple test concerning differences among means (one-way analysis of variance) can be used to ascertain whether social systems differ with regard to this variable. The question we want to answer is whether the extent of variation of a given characteristic within each country is smaller than variation among countries. If all trains in England move at a speed of 50 miles per hour and all trains in France move at a speed of 60 miles per hour, then knowing the fact that someone is traveling in France rather than in England will be helpful in predicting the duration of a journey. But if the speed of trains in both England and France varies between 30 and 70 miles per hour, the difference of 10 miles per hour in average speed may not be sufficient to improve a prediction about the duration of a trip. The type of train or time of the year may be much more important than the country.

The nature and the extent of intersocietal differences have long been subjects of theoretical formulations in the social sciences. Anthropologists tend to perceive societies as highly different. Although individual personalities are "potentially" the same, culture, social organization, child-rearing practices, or some other factors result in the predominance of certain personality types in particular societies. These cultural configurations, or "patterns of cultures," were originally identified from folk themes, customs, and so forth. Patterns of culture were not based on the notion of frequency distribution of personality types within a culture but on an ideal-type personality model. Subsequently, however, the concept of modal personality replaced the concept of patterns. Modal personality, defined as the product of interaction between "fundamental physiologically and neurologically determined tendencies and experiences common to all human beings" and their cultural milieu, became a subject of statistical analysis of distributions of personality types. Furthermore, if Singer's conclusions are correct, projective techniques indicate that the distributions within societies are flat, and within-culture differences of personalities are therefore larger than the between-culture differences.[18] It is not clear to what extent these findings can be generalized, but they are certainly surprising. Concepts of "cultural patterns," "modal personality," and "social character" and the problems of relating sociocultural settings to individual traits have an extensive theoretical tradition, but the empirical findings are scarce and thus inconclusive. As Inkeles and Levinson emphasize, "If national character refers to modes of a distribution of individual personality variants, then its study would seem to require the psychological investigation of adequately large and representative samples of persons, *studied individually.*"[19]

One set of attitudes that has been extensively studied concerns evaluations of occupational prestige in different societies.[20] Although the methodology of these studies has not been uniform and the samples have varied greatly, the general findings seem to indicate a high degree of inter-societal uniformity. These findings again run counter to our theoretical intuitions in light of which the prestige of occupations ought to be related to industrialization or social division of labor. But if the methodology of

[18] This discussion is based on Milton Singer, "A Survey of Culture and Personality Theory and Research," in Bert Kaplan, ed., *Studying Personality Cross Culturally,* Row, Peterson, Evanston, Ill., 1961.

[19] Cited in Singer, *op. cit.,* p. 55.

[20] Alex Inkeles and Peter Rossi, "National Comparisons of Occupational Prestige, *American Journal of Sociology,* **61**, 1956; Alex Inkeles, "Industrial Man: The Relation of Status to Experience, Perception, and Value," *American Journal of Sociology,* **66**, 1961; E. M. Thomas, "Reinspecting a Structural Position on Occupational Prestige," *American Journal of Sociology,* **67**, 1962; A. O. Haller, D. I. Lewis, and Iwao Ishino, "The Hypothesis of Intersocietal Similarity in Occupational Prestige Hierarchies," *American Journal of Sociology,* **71**, 1966. Research reports on occupational status are available from at least 16 countries.

these studies is sound—if Americans and Japanese, Poles and Brazilians, Germans and Indonesians evaluate particular occupations alike—theories relating the socioeconomic structure to these attitudes will have to be revised. Social science theories may in general overstate intersocietal differences and the role of system-level factors, and in this era of empirical truth many myths might have to be revised. When Lipset and Bendix stated that "the overall pattern of social mobility appears to be much the same in the industrial societies of various Western countries," they felt it necessary to emphasize that this finding "runs counter to widely help impressions concerning the different social structures of American and Western European societies."[21]

If no differences are found among systems, the population is homogeneous and systemic factors cannot be expected to be important as determinants. Thus the test of differences between or among national means—either a mean test or a variance test—provides a general estimate of the relevance of systemic factors and a guideline for the choice of the proper level of analysis. If the sample is differentiated in terms of systemic characteristics, generalizations beyond the examined sample of countries seem relatively safe. If the Indian, Polish, Yugoslav, and American local leaders do not differ in their orientation toward change, it can be expected that local leaders in other countries are not significantly different, and, in general, that systemic factors are not important in explaining this particular attitude.

These examples of intersystemic similarities with regard to a single phenomenon, such as personality types, evaluation of occupations, social mobility, or values of local leaders, are by no means intended to support a thesis that social systems do not differ. Illustrations, both of an impressionistic and systematic nature, of intersystemic differences are abundant. The examples discussed were merely intended to show that the assumption of intersystemic similarities, underlying the most different systems design, should not be discarded a priori as invalid. To our surprise and contrary to many theories, such similarities are indeed being discovered. The validity of this assumption, of course, will depend upon the nature of the social phenomena under consideration: one may expect that psychophysiological phenomena will be less dependent upon the social system than are political phenomena.

A limitation on comparing systems with regard to individual-level phenomena must be emphasized: the problems of measurement. Cross-system comparisons of single variables will be dependent upon the units and the scale of measurement within each social system. Very often such direct

[21] S. M. Lipset and Reinhard Bendix, *Social Mobility in Industrial Society,* University of California Press, Berkeley, 1960, pp. 11 and 13.

comparisons will not be possible, either because the scales of measurement are unknown (e.g., is political participation in the Soviet Union higher than in the United States?) or because the investigator may choose to quantify the variables in a way that precludes this kind of comparisons (e.g., by dichotomizing at the national medians). This limitation will be discussed in greater detail in Part Two.

Comparing Relationships

Descriptive, univariate comparisons may often not only be difficult, they may also be less interesting than the multivariate patterns of determination. Since most theoretical propositions are formulated in terms of predicting one variable by some other variables, the form and the fit of these predictions are of central importance for a theoretically minded social scientist. Within-system predictions and the fit of these predictions, or "relationships," often constitute the focus of analysis. When leaders and citizens in several countries are studied, one can ask whether membership in India or Yugoslavia has more effect on the values of an individual than a position as a local leader. When perceived freedom to discuss politics is studied, one can ask whether education or the system better predicts individual perceptions. If achievement motivation is studied in Brazil and in the United States, one can ask whether social class or nationality is a better predictor.

The question is whether the relationship between the variable being explained and an independent variable is the same within all systems: whether systemic characteristics are important in determining the form and the fit of theoretical predictions in different social systems. Again, if values in all countries are in the same way associated with political positions, or if freedom to discuss politics is related to education, or achievement motivation to social class, then systemic factors are not important in explaining the dependent variable. And again, as additional independent variables are considered, it may very likely transpire that at some point systemic characteristics do influence the observed relationships. But each finding of similarity of relationships across social systems reduces the number of potentially relevant systemic characteristics. The most different systems design implies an analytical strategy in which the overall influence of systemic factors is assessed step-by-step with the addition of each new variable.

Illustrations of similar relationships in various social systems are plentiful. Most recent comparative studies of political behavior seem to discover that relationships among individual attitudes are the same regardless of political system. In his inventory of research on political participation, Milbrath found only two instances in which a relationship was not the same in all political systems.[22] The study of civic culture consistently shows that education is the most powerful determinant of political attitudes in five countries. Indeed, Almond and Verba conclude the following:

"It is . . . among the most important facts we discovered that most of the relationships between education and political orientation are of the first type: educational groups differ from one another substantially, and in a similar way, in each nation.[23]

Rokkan reports similar findings in the study of attitudes toward European integration:

". . . Gallup International, in its study of *Public Opinion and the Europe of the Six,* found that 62 percent of the Dutch sample was strongly in favor of unification, and only 36 percent of the Italians. This difference, however, tells us very little about the chances of strains between the two countries in the articulation of policies toward Europe. It turns out that the *better educated in the two national samples think practically alike*: 70 percent of them were strongly in favor of European unification. The difference between the two countries resulted almost entirely from a contrast in levels of education and information. . . . [emphasis added]"[24]

Converse and Dupeux report major differences in the frequency of party identification between France and the United States. Seventy-five percent of Americans identify themselves with a political party, while only 45 percent of the Frenchmen perceive themselves in partisan terms. This difference, however, can be attributed to the higher rates of political socialization through the family in the United States. The authors show that in both countries those persons who know their father's party preference are very likely to have a party preference themselves—79.4 percent in France and 81.6 in the United States. Converse and Dupeux conclude:

"Where the socialization processes have been the same in the two societies, the results in current behavior appear to be the same, in rates of formation of identification. The strong cross-national differences lie in the socialization processes. In other words, we have come full circle again: we

[22] L. W. Milbrath, *Political Participation,* Rand McNally, Chicago, 1965.

[23] G. A. Almond and Sidney Verba, *op. cit.,* p. 317.

[24] Stein Rokkan, "Comparative Cross-National Research: The Context of Current Efforts," in R. L. Merritt and Stein Rokkan, eds., *Comparing Nations: the Use of Quantitative Data in Cross-National Research,* Yale University Press, New Haven, Conn., 1966, p. 19.

have encountered large national differences but have once again succeeded in moving them to the marginals of the table."[25]

One could expect that in all the cases cited above the social system does not increase the accuracy of prediction of the dependent variable. If an illiterate Italian were an illiterate Dutchman, his attitude toward integration would have been the same. If an American who does not know his father's party preference were a Frenchman who did not know his preference, it would still be unlikely that he would have party identification. As long as the independent variables remain the same, membership in a social system is not important in predicting the dependent variable. Education is a good predictor; social system is not. Class is a good predictor; social system is not. What matters is not whether an individual's name is John Smith or Giovanni Bianco, but whether he went to school or not, whether he knows his father's party preference or not, whether he has a high income or not. The countries differ with regard to their levels of education, class structure, and family socialization, but they do not differ as *systems* so long as their patterns of relationships are the same. *Systems differ not when the frequency of particular characteristics differ, but when the patterns of the relationships among variables differ.*[26]

The fact that a single independent variable measured within systems yields a gain in prediction of the dependent phenomenon does not preclude the possibility that systems may *also* contribute to the explanation. If a set of independent variables, measured wthin each system, predicts the dependent phenomenon independently of *all* systemic characteristics, the initial variation of the dependent variable will disappear when the means of the independent variables are adjusted. If the difference between Americans and Frenchmen disappears when the frequency of knowledge of father's party identification is adjusted, then systems cannot contribute to the

[25] P. E. Converse and Georges Dupeux, "Politicization of the Electorate in France and the United States," in L. A. Coser, ed., *Political Sociology*, Harper & Row, New York, 1966, pp. 233–34.

[26] A large number of examples of the structure of relationships among attitudes can be seen in several studies attempting to develop attitude-measuring instruments. These findings are most impressive in that, in spite of the difference among the cultures and the differences in the intensiey of particular attitudes, the *structure* of interrelationships among attitudes is highly invariant. See, for example, D. H. Smith and Alex Inkeles, "The OM Scale: A Comparative Socio-Psychological Measure of Individual Modernity," *Sociometry*, **29**, 1966; J. A. Kahl, "Some Measurements of Achievement Orientation," *American Journal of Sociology*, **70**, 1965; Howard Maclay and E. E. Ware, "Cross-Cultural Use of the Semantic Differential," *Behavioral Science*, **6**, 1961; Salomon Rettig and Benjamin Pasamanick, "Invariance in Factor Structure of Moral Value Judgments from American and Korean College Students," *Sociometry*, **29**, 1966.

explanation. If, however, the difference of achievement motivation between Americans and Brazilians does not disappear—if both class *and* nationality have an effect on achievement motivation—then further analysis must follow. Rosen found that both social class and nationality have an effect on the age at which achievement training is seen as proper, that social class is much more important than nationality for the age of independence training, and that nationality is more important than social class for actual achievement motivation scores. The system is an important predictor of achievement scores; it is less important than social class for predicting the age when independence training takes place; and it is as important as social class for predicting the age when achievement training takes place.[27]

In general, when a relationship between two variables is found to be the same across social systems, the number of systemic characteristics operating on the dependent variable is reduced. The systemic factors, however, are not completely eliminated from further explanation. If and only if initial variation of the dependent variable disappears when independent variables are adjusted in each system can systemic factors completely be disregarded. But, if at some stage of analysis systems do yield a gain in prediction, systemic factors must be considered. Such cases will be discussed in the following chapter.

[27] B. C. Rosen, "Socialization and Achievement Motivation in Brazil," *American Sociological Review,* 27, 1962.

CHAPTER THREE

System Level Variables: Changing the Level of Analysis

Differing Relationships. Comparative Study and Levels of Analysis.
System-Level Variables: Diffusion Patterns, Settings, and Contexts.
Level of Analysis and Inference: Interpreting Ecological Correlations.
Inferences when Within-System Relationships are Similar.
Inferences when Within-System Relationships Differ Systematically.
Conclusion.

Differing Relationships

It should be clear from the preceding chapter that whenever the within-system relationships are sufficiently different, identification of the social system will improve explanation. When systemic factors are introduced, the level of analysis is changed. Problems involved in this change constitute the topic of this chapter.

The most simple case requiring a change of level of analysis occurs when a bivariate relationship is different in two or more systems. Bendix and Lipset cite several such cases concerning political behavior of various occupational groups. For example, they report the following:

"Among workers in Germany and Sweden, the better paid and more skilled are more likely to be class-conscious, and vote social democratic or communist, than those who are less well paid and less skilled. In Britain, the United States, and Australia, however, the lower paid and less skilled proved better supporters of left parties than do the upper strata of the working class."[1]

We also know that teachers and physicians are further to the right than other professionals in Germany, while they are further to the left in France and Britain. Workers have a lower rate of political participation than people with higher incomes in the United States and Britain, but a higher rate in France. Upwardly mobile persons in the United States tend to be more conservative than those who retain the social position of their fathers, whereas in several European countries mobile persons are less conservative. Alker demonstrates that the correlation between achievement motivation and per capita income is positive in Latin America and negative in the European countries.[2] Almond and Verba indicate that the correlation between church attendance and party identification is almost nonexistent in the United States, while it is highly negative in Italy and Mexico.[3] Dogan shows that the relationship between land ownership and Communist voting among poor peasants is positive in France but negative in Italy.[4] Janowitz et al. demonstrate that the intensity of class-based political cleavages is significantly higher in Great Britain than in the United States.[5]

In all of these examples "systems differ." But to say that systems differ is to say that some characteristic that distinguishes these systems influences the observed relationships. Whenever identification of particular social systems contributes to explanation, one must ask what it is about these systems that influences the phenomenon being explained. What is it about Germany and Sweden, on the one hand, and Great Britain, the United States, and Australia, on the other, that makes skilled workers behave differently in politics? What is it about the Latin American and European countries that determines the different relationships between achievement motivation and per capita income? What distinguishes the group of countries where the relationship between level of economic development and domestic violence is negative from another group where the relationship is positive?

[1] Reinhard Bendix and S. M. Lipset, "The Field of Political Sociology," in L. A. Coser, ed., *Political Sociology*, Harper & Row, New York, 1966, p. 32.

[2] H. R. Alker, "The Comparison of Aggregate Political and Social Data: Potentialities and Problems," *Social Science Information*, 5, 1966.

[3] G. A. Almond and Sidney Verba, *The Civic Culture*, Princeton University Press, Princeton, N.J., 1963.

[4] Mattei Dogan, "Political Cleavage and Social Stratification in France and Italy," in S. M. Lipset and Stein Rokkan, eds., *Party Systems and Voter Alignments: Cross-National Perspectives*, Free Press, New York, 1967.

[5] Morris Janowitz, Klaus Liepelt, and D. R. Segal, "An Approach to the Comparative Analysis of Political Partisanship," an unpublished paper, no date.

Comparative Study and Levels of Analysis

The questions posed above concern the impact of systemic characteristics on the behavior of individuals within those systems. All the questions are based on an assumption that the dependent variable is measured within systems, and therefore systemic factors enter the theory only as independent variables. However, not all studies conducted in several systems are based on this kind of design. Some simple designs based on the number of levels of analysis and the nature of the dependent variable will be discussed.

1. All variables, dependent and independent, *are observed at the same level*. Neither aggregation nor analysis of within-system relationships is possible. Survey research usually involves this kind of design: individuals are the only units of analysis. But studies conducted exclusively at the level of countries also share this design. This is true, for example, when democracy measured by judgmental classification is related to the level of economic development.

2. Some variables are observed within systems and some are observed at the level of systems, but *analysis is confined exclusively to the cross-systemic level*. Thus some of the variables constitute aggregates of individual characteristics, and other variables are observed directly at the level of systems. If the dependent variable is observed directly at the level of systems, research concerns the impact of individual behaviors on the behavior of systems. Huntington's theory of institutionalization requires this kind of design since the theory concerns the impact of political mobilization of individuals on the institutionalization of the political system.[6] If the variables observed at the level of systems are the independent variables, research concerns the impact of systems on the behavior of individuals within them. For example, what is the effect of interparty competition on voting turnout [7] or the effect of an "authoritarian culture" on the degree of authoritarianism of individuals?[8] Even though individuals are observed within systems, their properties, such as age or literacy, are aggregated and treated as system level variables. The resulting findings relate "an average person" within a system or a "part of the population" of a system to some characteristics of the system. Levels of observation are multiple, but the analysis is conducted only at one level.

[6] S. P. Huntington, "Political Development and Political Decay," *World Politics,* **17**, 1965.

[7] For example, Dawson reports a correlation of circa .60 (Gamma) between interparty competition and voting turnout in the American states. R. E. Dawson, "Social Development, Party Competition and Policy," in W. N. Chambers and W. D. Burnham, eds., *The American Party Systems,* Oxford University Press, New York, 1967.

[8] E. T. Prothro and Lenov H. Melikian, "The California Public Opinion Scale in an Authoritarian Culture," *Public Opinion Quarterly,* **17**, 1953.

3. Variables are observed at multiple levels, and the *analysis is conducted at multiple levels.* It is not necessary for any characteristics to be observed directly at the level of systems because system-level analysis may investigate the influence of within-system distributions on individual behavior. Ordinarily, however, some variables will be observed at the system level. If the dependent variable is a phenomenon observed at the level of systems, the research concerns the impact of the patterns of relationships within systems on the behavior of the system. For example, Hoselitz argues that if the income of individuals is related to their prestige, then the system will develop economically.[9] Feierabend shows that if individual expectations exceed individual satisfaction, a system will be unstable.[10] If the dependent variable is observed at a within-system level, then the question concerns the impact of the system on the pattern of relationships within it. For example, the presence of a poll tax will tend to increase the relationship between income and voting. This is the typical paradigm of explanation in the "functional" analysis. When a system is in a state that is not an "equilibrium state," some structures become activated to bring the system back to equilibrium. Thus a property of the system—being in a nonequilibrium state—is used to explain a behavior of the elements of the system.

Although all of the above examples were formulated at the level of individuals and countries, these designs can be applied regardless of what the levels of observation and analysis are. For example, the design of the International Studies of Values in Politics involved the study of the values of individual local leaders and of institutional behavior of local communities[1.1] Individual values were aggregated at the community level within each country. Questions were subsequently asked about the impact of country-level variables, such as degree of autonomy of local governments, upon the relationship between values of leaders and the "activeness" of the community within each country. Thus the study employed triple levels of observation—individuals, communities, and countries—and double levels of analysis—community and country.

In comparative research, we are concerned with studies in which analysis proceeds at multiple levels. Even if the levels of observation are multiple but the levels of analysis are not, such studies will not be considered as "comparative." In other words, we are only concerned with studies in

[9] B. F. Hoselitz, *Sociological Aspects of Economic Growth,* Free Press, Glencoe, Ill., 1960.

[10] I. K. Feierabend and R. L. Feierabend, "Aggressive Behavior within Politics, 1948–1962: A Cross-National Study," *Journal of Conflict Resolution,* **10,** 1966.

[11] P. E. Jacob, Henry Teune, and T. M. Watts, "Values, Leadership, and Development," *Social Science Information,* **7,** 1968.

which both the patterns of relationships within each system and the role of systemic factors are examined.

System-Level Variables: Diffusion Patterns, Settings, and Contexts

In order to discover what it is about systems that influences the behavior of individuals within them, we must first distinguish among types of characteristics of systems. Locating these types is particularly important since the number of systemic factors associated with differences in the patterns of relationships is always larger than the number of systems that can be observed. If some rules were available to determine at least what *type* of systemic characteristics operate on the dependent variable, the number of potentially explanatory system-level variables could be reduced. It should be emphasized that our attempt to distinguish among various types of systemic factors is not identical with the attempts to classify, conceptually or empirically, "group properties"[12] or "dimensions of nations."[13] We are concerned only with factors that may potentially influence or be influenced by within-system behaviors, not with properties of systems as potential variables in system- or group-level analyses.

To say that a group of social systems shares a certain characteristic that in turn distinguishes it from some other systems is to specify one of three types of systemic factors, which will be called "diffusion patterns," "settings," and "contexts."

1. *Diffusion Patterns.*[14] One interpretation of the similarity of political behavior of skilled workers in Anglo-Saxon countries may be that this behavior is a result of the diffusion of a cultural pattern. The relationship between occupation and political-attitudes is not based on independent events—neither the social nor the political system of the Anglo-Saxon countries influences the skilled workers to be conservative and the unskilled workers to be leftist. In this interpretation, rather, the relationship is a result of historical learning.

This problem, known in anthropology as "Galton's problem," has been

---

[12] P. F. Lazersfeld and Morris Rosenberg, *The Language of Social Research,* Free Press, Glencoe, Ill., 1955, Section IV.

[13] R. J. Rummel, "The Dimensionality of Nations Project," in R. L. Merritt and Stein Rokkan, eds., *Comparing Nations,* Yale University Press, New Haven, Conn., 1963; P. M. Gregg and A. S. Banks, "Dimensions of Political Systems: Factor Analysis of a Cross-Polity Survey," *American Political Science Review,* **59**, 1965.

[14] We thank Professor Raoul Naroll for making us aware of this problem.

discussed several times by Naroll.[15] Statistically the question is how many independent events can we observe? If the similarity within a group of systems is a result of diffusion, there is only one independent observation, and the number of degrees of freedom is zero. Naroll cites some fascinating examples of such situations:

"Klimek shows that in aboriginal California, patrilinear totemic clans are to be found invariably and exclusively in tribes (of the southeast corner of the state) which also play tunes on flageolets, use carrying frames made of sticks and cords, make oval plate pottery, use a squared muller, and favor twins. ... Debt slavery was practical only in the northwest corner of the present state . . . [and it is] found invariably and exclusively among the tribes whose women wear flat caps made of overlay twined basketry, whose men wear painted deerskin capes, who cook in low cooking baskets, who use pipes inlaid with haliotis and who levy a fine for adultery."[16]

Several solutions designed to determine whether a pattern of relationships is a result of diffusion or "functional" interdependence were proposed by Naroll.[17] All of these solutions, however, are based on the assumption that geographical proximity determines communication among cultures. It is doubtful whether this assumption is as useful in the study of modern societies as it is with regard to primitive cultures.

Problems of determining whether what is observed is a diffusion pattern or a functional relationship are frequent and important to other social sciences as well as anthropology. A classical controversy of this nature concerns the meaning of the Weberian hypothesis relating Protestant values to capitalist orientations. Is it a "functional" proposition that a person who is a Protestant will be more likely than a Catholic to be an entrepreneur or that Protestant countries are more likely than Catholic countries to de-

---

[15] Raoul Naroll, "Galton's Problem: The Logic of Cross-Cultural Analysis," *Social Research*, **32**, 1965.

[16] *Ibid.*, pages 434–35.

[17] For the specific solutions see Raoul Naroll, "Two Solutions to Galton's Problem," *Philosophy of Science*, **28**, 1961; Raoul Naroll and R. G. D'Andrade, "Two Further Solutions to Galton's Problem," *American Anthropologist*, **65**, 1963; and Raoul Naroll, "A Fifth Solution to Galton's Problem," *American Anthropologist*, **66**, 1964.

velop economically?[18] Or is the Weberian hypothesis really a description of a unique historical event that took place once when an expanding system of religious values turned people to earthly preoccupations? Similar questions are raised with respect to evaluations of occupational prestige. Are they a function of the division of labor in a society or of exposure to a foreign system of values that is gradually adopted as societies go through the process of functional differentiation?[19] Do Indonesian high school students evaluate occupations in the same way as Americans because their social structure resembles that of the United States or because they are learning a system of values broadcast by the United States Information Agency? Such questions become even more acute in studies of social change. Does change take place because transformations took place within a country or because the country was exposed to some values and behaviors originating from an alien source? Is economic development a function of internal changes or external exposure? How many times did economic development take place spontaneously—whenever a country passed some threshold of structural changes or only once, when the first pattern was formed?[20]

No general solutions to these problems are readily available. If we had a chance to observe some social systems that were not exposed to external communication, the impact of diffusion could be assessed. But, as Levi-Strauss convinces us, no primitive culture can resist exposure to the "modern" world.[21] When contact is established, only one civilization survives. Precise statistical controls could compare amounts of foreign contacts with internal transformations. But whether we will be ever able to determine whether "a society changed" or "a society was absorbed" remains doubtful.

2. *Settings.* A second type of system properties consists of characteristics that are neither diffusional patterns nor aggregates of observations.

[18] H. H. Anderson and G. L. Anderson, "Cultural Reactions to Conflict: A Study of Adolescent Children in Seven Countries," in G. M. Gilbert, ed., *Psychological Approaches to Intergroup and International Understanding,* University of Texas, Austin, 1956. The authors compared Protestant and Catholic children with regard to concern over money and showed that Protestants are indeed more concerned about money than Catholics. But whether this is a test of Weber's theory is questionable.

[19] Zygmunt Bauman, "Social Concomitants of Economic Development," a paper presented at the UNESCO Conference on Social Prerequisites to Economic Growth, Kyrenia, Cyprus, April, 1963.

[20] For a view arguing that development took place spontaneously and as a result of indigenous conditions only once and that subsequent developments in other countries were a result of adaptation of foreign patterns, see W. Kula, *Problemy i Metody Historii Gospodarczej,* Panstwowe Wydawnictwo Naukowe,Warsaw, 1964.

[21] C. Levi-Strauss, *Tristes Tropiques,* Atheneum Publishers, New York, 1969.

These characteristics cannot be observed at the level of individuals. They correspond to what Lazersfeld and Rosenberg call "global" characteristics [22] although they are treated here in broader terms than Cattell's "syntality" variables.[23] Settings constitute characteristics to which all individuals within a system are, at least potentially, exposed. Settings may be (1) historical, (2) institutional, (3) external, (4) behavioral, and (5) physical.

All individuals within a social system may be affected by the past history of that system. For example, it is important for the present political behavior of individuals whether universal suffrage was extended before or after education became universal.[24] We find that the number of years a country has been independent, the number of years the same constitution has been in operation, or the average length of time a chief executive or a party has been in office may influence the present behavior of individuals within a system.[25] Such historical factors may not only directly affect the behavior of individuals, but may also influence properties of the system that in turn affect individual behavior. A particularly interesting example of a quantitative application of a historical-setting variable is presented by Allardt, who shows that the number of persons who were killed in a Finnish commune during the civil war of 1918–21 is related to votes for the Communist party in that commune today.[26]

Institutional-setting factors are used extensively in political science. An old controversy between political sociologists and political scientists concerned the question of the impact of institutional factors on individual political behavior. Sociologists, naturally, tend to seek socioeconomic determinants of political behavior, whereas political scientists tend to look at institutional characteristics such as constitutions. The focus of this controversy centered on the relative importance of socioeconomic and institutional factors in influencing party systems and voting behavior.[27] Rae's study of the political consequences of electoral laws is an empirical attempt

[22] Lazersfeld and Rosenberg, *op. cit.,* p. 287.

[23] R. B. Cattell, "Types of Group Characteristics," in Lazersfeld and Rosenberg, *op. cit.*

[24] Reinhard Bendix and Stein Rokkan, "The Extension of National Citizenship to the Lower Classes: A Comparative Perspective," a paper presented to the Fifth World Congress of Sociology, Washington, 1962.

[25] For example, D. A. Rustow, *A World of Nations,* The Brookings Institution, Washington, D.C., 1967.

[26] Erik Allardt, "Patterns of Class Conflict and Working Class Consciousness in Finnish Politics," Publications of the Institute of Sociology, University of Helsinki, No. 30, 1964.

[27] For example, S. M. Lipset, "Party Systems and Representation of Social Groups," Institute of Industrial Relations, University of California, Berkeley, 1961.

to determine the importance of institutional-setting factors.[28] Rae finds that, although the effect of the electoral laws on distribution of seats is only marginal, these effects are nonetheless sufficient to produce important political consequences. Analyses of the influence of institutions on individual behavior are numerous, but not unambiguous. All Americans have only one president, at least at one point of time, and to this extent the properties of this office and of the person who occupies it may be important in explaining individual behavior. The degree of centralization of the educational system, the extent of economic planning, the degree of autonomy of local governments—all such factors may be important as determinants of the behavior of individuals within a system. Institutional-setting variables are deceptively easy to assess, and this often leads to misleading inferences from institutions to behaviors, either of systems or individuals within them. For example, the number of parties has been frequently used to indicate interparty competition, democracy, opposition, and participation. However, it is still not clear what effect, if any, the number of parties actually has on the behavior of individuals.

External relations of a system may influence the behavior of individuals within it and vice versa. Several studies attempt to relate internal and external conflict. It seems that internal sociopsychological conflict but not political conflict is related to the external conflict of a system.[29]

The behavior of a system or any of its subsystems may have an impact on or be influenced by the behavior of individuals within it. Lipset argues that if the political system is effective, it will gain legitimacy in the eyes of its members.[30] Interparty competition has a different effect on voting participation in different systems.[31] Conversely, behavior of individuals may influence the behavior of the system. Huntington's theory perceives institutionalization as a function of relationships among individual behavior within a system. Marx's theories systematically formulate the influence of

[28] Douglas Rae, *The Political Consequences of Electoral Laws,* Yale University Press, New Haven, Conn., 1967.

[29] R. J. Rummel, "Testing Some Possible Predictors of Conflict Within and Between Nations," *Peace Research Society, Papers,* 1, 1964; Michael Haas, "Social Change and National Aggressiveness, 1900–1960," in J. D. Singer, ed., *Quantitative International Politics,* Free Press, New York, 1967.

[30] S. M. Lipset, *Political Man,* Doubleday, New York, 1960.

[31] American findings show that when the degree of interparty competition is high, more people turn out to vote. Like many other findings from American research, this one seems to be of a general nature. But Allardt indicates that in Finland more people vote in those communes in which one of the parties is safely dominant, unless it is the Social Democratic Party. See Erik Allardt and Pertti Pesonen, "Cleavages in Finnish Politics," in S. M. Lipset and Stein Rokkan, eds., *Party Systems and Voter Alignments, op. cit.*

interrelations of individuals on the change of a system. But in general such theories are scarce.

The last type of setting variables consists of properties of a physical nature. These variables may concern some characteristics of the physical or material environment or some physical characteristics of a society. Physical and material characteristics such as resources, accumulated capital, and the like, are used most frequently in economics and to some extent in anthropology when a culture is described in terms of the influence of physical environment on individuals.

3. *Contexts.* Within each social system, individuals hold certain attitudes and interact both with each other and with their physical environment. When the characteristics of individuals—whether predispositional, behavioral, or relational—are aggregated, the social system of which they are members acquires a parameter. Context factors constitute aggregates of individual characteristics. A useful distinction among context factors is that which Cattell calls "structural" and "population" variables.[32] Structural contexts are aggregates of relational properties; population contexts are aggregates of individual properties.

Structural contexts are system-level variables generalized from individual characteristics in which "a reference is needed either to other members of the unit or the unit as a whole."[33] Although the question of whether structural variables can be reduced to individual attributes is controversial, and in fact structural variables are rarely formed by simple aggregation when systems are large, one can view structural contexts such as division of labor, class structure, income inequality, and communication flow as aggregates of individual relations within a system. To say that the division of labor within a system is high is to aggregate observations about any two persons sharing an occupation. To characterize income inequality is to generalize the distance between incomes of pairs of persons. To state that a system has a dense communication network is to generalize a matrix describing individual interactions. Although these structural contexts can be observed and measured directly, if structure is viewed as a generalization of relations among individuals within a system, it is in principle observable at the within-system level. Therefore they constitute a context rather than a setting.

Population contexts are intuitively clear. They constitute aggregates of individual characteristics, whether they are predispositional or behavioral.

[32] Cattell, "Types of Group Characteristics," *op. cit.*
[33] P. L. Kendall and P. F. Lazersfeld, "The Relation between Individual and Group Characteristics in *The American Soldier"* in Lazersfeld and Rosenberg, *op. cit.,* p. 293.

For example, Turks are on the average more achievement-oriented than Iranians; Frenchmen are less frequently identified with a political party than Americans; Syrian students are more authoritarian than American students. All of these observations are expressed either as means, based on some units of measurement assumed to be common across systems, or as proportions of populations in which an individual is the unit of measurement and the attributes are dichotomous. The measurement of contextual variables presents several serious problems that will be discussed in Part Two.

For system description or analytical studies conducted exclusively at the system level, the importance of contextual variables is evident. But since we are concerned here with system-level factors as determinants or consequences of within-system behavior, their role may be much more limited. In comparative studies it is not sufficient to characterize the average authoritarianism of Syrian students, the party identification of American voters, or the achievement motivation of Turks. Nor is it sufficient to identify the extent to which an average Indian is poorer or richer than other Indians or the extent to which an average Brazilian shares his occupation with other Brazilians. If a system attribute is to be treated as a system-level variable in comparative terms, it must be demonstrated that some characteristic of the distribution of the individual attributes influences individual behavior within the system. Does the fact that a system has a certain property influence the individuals within it? Although over 90 percent of the population of Ghana is black, at any one point of time this does not affect the color of the skin of individual Ghanians. Only 50 percent of the population of Brazil is literate. If the percentage of literates is to be treated as a system-level variable rather than just as an aggregate descriptor, however, it must be demonstrated empirically that it affects some attribute of individual Brazilians. It is not sufficient for comparative purposes to state the aggregate parameter of a system. It is necessary to treat it as a potential determinant of behaviors at a different level of analysis.

Level of Analysis and Inference: Interpreting Ecological Correlations

Comparative studies involve a population derived from "natural" groupings of individuals such as societies, economies, polities, or cultures. This population is sampled in a two-step fashion: systems are selected first and individuals or other units within them next. Relationships among variables can be analyzed *within* each system. But when individual characteristics are aggregated, these relations are also observable at the level of systems. In other words, for any set of variables measured within each system, three types of predictions can be made: (1) *Individual values* of the dependent variable can be predicted from the *individual values* of the independent variables on the basis of regressions *within particular systems* ("within-systems regression"). (2) *System means* of the dependent variable can be predicted from *system means* of the independent variables on the basis of regression *across systems* ("among-system regression"). (3) *Individual values* of the dependent variable can be predicted from the *individual values* of the independent variables on the basis of regression *common to the entire population of individuals,* regardless of the social system involved ("total regression").

Although many regression analyses in the social sciences are not guided by a theory, any prediction of a functional dependence of one variable on other variables should be derived from a theory. It is not sufficient to hypothesize that *"X is related to Y."* A "relationship" can almost never be assessed in the absence of a prediction. A relationship, as measured by correlation coefficients, has meaning only in terms of the fit of a prediction that has a specific functional form. With regard to interval data, the most frequent assumption is that the function describing the dependence of two variables is linear, that is, that it generates a straight line. A linear prediction states that any change of the independent variable by a fixed interval is accompanied by a constant change in the dependent variable. If the independent variable changes by one unit, the dependent variable is different by **b** units. Coefficient **b,** usually called the "regression coefficient," describes, therefore, the magnitude of differences in the dependent variable corresponding to a difference of one unit in the values of the independent variable. "Regression intercept," usually symbolized by **a,** shows the value of the dependent variable when the independent variables equal zero. Thus in the case of two variables, the regression equation generating a straight line has the following general form:

$$y_i = a + bx_i,$$

where *i* varies along units of observation.

For reasons discussed in the Introduction, however, we cannot expect that this prediction will be deterministic. Even a larger number of independent variables will rarely predict every single value of the dependent variable. For each value of the independent variable, *X,* we expect to find some (constant) amount of variation of the dependent variable, *Y.* The larger the amount of variance of the *Y's* about their least-square linear regression on *X,* the worse is the fit of prediction and the lower is the linear relationship between *X* and *Y.* But even if the variance of Y's around their linear regression on *X* is equal to the total variance of *Y's* about their mean, that is, even when *b* equals zero and the best-fitting linear regression coincides with the mean, one cannot conclude that "there is no relationship" between *X* and *Y*. A simple quadratic function may still provide an ideal fit, and thus there may be a perfect curvilinear relationship between the two variables. A form of prediction is logically primary to its fit, or relationship.[34] The amount of variance about the linear least-square equation is measured by product-moment correlation coefficient. The square of this coefficient tells us what percentage of the total variance of the dependent variable is predicted by its linear regression on the independent variables. Thus correlation is a measure of fit of prediction. Underlying the subsequent discussion will be the assumption that the variances of both the dependent and the independent variables do not vary greatly from system to system and, thus, that differences in the slopes of within-system regressions are proportional to differences of their fit. A relationship will mean a fit of a linear least-square equation relative to constant variances of both variables.

The total relationship between two variables, each observed within a number of systems, equals a sum of the relationships within systems and the relationship of system means. In other words, the fit of the total regression can be expressed as a sum, with appropriate weights, of the fits of regressions within particular systems and of the regression of means. More precisely, it is the total covariance that is equal to a weighted sum of within- and between-systems covariances. Covariance is the average product of the simultaneous deviations of two variables from their respective means, or, in other terms, it is the product of the correlation between two variables and their respective standard deviations.

Since in comparative research all three types of regression can be analyzed, it is possible that three different relationships will be found. The relationship between race and illiteracy may be nonexistent *within* each American state, but it may be highly positive when the percentages of Negroes and of illiterates are examined in each state or region. The relationship between industrialization and Communist voting may be found to be negative at the level of countries but positive when administrative districts within countries are used as units of analysis. In general, what inferences can be made on the basis of comparing the within-system relationships, the relationship of system means, and the total relationship?

Much has been said about this problem, although in a somewhat different context. The problem was identified in Robinson's article as "ecological

---

[34] A reader who needs further explanation of regression should consult a basic statistics textbook, such as H. M. Blalock, *Social Statistics*, McGraw-Hill, New York, 1960.

correlation."[35] He pointed out that inferences about individual-level relationships drawn from relationships between aggregated parameters may be fallacious. The force of this warning has been weakened, both by Goodman's reformulation of the problem as one of comparing regressions [36] and by the increasing interest in theoretical interpretations of ecological correlations. The problem is not to list the "fallacies" involved in making cross-level inferences, but to interpret theoretically the observed differences between individual and ecological correlations. As Duncan, Cuzzort, and Duncan argued, "correlations in which the units of observation are areal units are by no means always computed merely as an inferior substitute for the theoretically preferable individual correlations. . . ."[37] Blalock demonstrated that a change in the level of analysis involves a change in the system of variables operating on the dependent phenomenon. As he has stated, "In shifting from one unit of analysis to another we are very likely to affect the manner in which outside and possibly disturbing influences are operating on the dependent and independent variables under consideration."[38] Most of Blalock's subsequent discussion however, deals with artificially created groupings, whereas our focus is on the naturally formed units.

Inferences when Within-System Relationships are Similar

Decisions concerning the proper level of analysis and the type of system-level factors that should be considered depend upon the difference between the within-systems regressions, the regression of means, and the total regression for the pooled population. In the clearest case, within-system regressions would all have the same slope and would share it with the total regression.

In this situation the relationships are the same within particular systems, and the prediction based on the within-system regressions does not differ from the prediction based on the regression of the means. Systemic factors clearly do not have to be taken into consideration since the form and the fit of predictions is the same regardless of social system.

For example, let us assume that in several countries the extent of inter-party competition in an electoral district is positively related to voting

[35] W. S. Robinson, "Ecological Correlations and the Behavior of Individuals," *American Sociological Review,* **15**, 1950.

[36] L. A. Goodman, "Ecological Regressions and Behavior of Individuals," *American Sociological Review,* **18**, 1953.

[37] O. D. Duncan, R. P. Cuzzort, and B. Duncan, *Statistical Geography,* Free Press, New York, 1961, p. 27.

[38] H. M. Blalock, *Causal Inferences in Nonexperimental Research,* University of North Carolina, Chapel Hill, 1964, p. 98.

turnout. Wherever the competition is high, voting turnout tends to be high. If this relationship is similar in all countries under study and if a similar relationship is discovered when the extent of competition and turnout are aggregated for each system, all three regressions will have a similar slope. In this situation a single general statement can be formulated, according to which these two variables are positively related. There is no need to concern ourselves with the problems of ecological inferences.

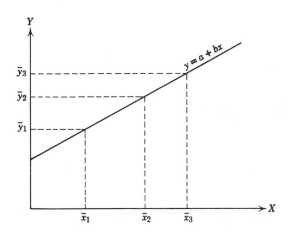

Figure **1**

In other situations, however, either the within-system regressions—the same in particular systems—differ from the regression based on the means or the within-system regressions are not the same. An interpretation of these differences will be helpful in elucidating the nature of the systemic factors influencing the dependent variable. We will discuss later a few situations in which the difference between the within- and the between-system regressions is theoretically interpretable, rather than develop general rules for making inferences. The discussion will be restricted to two variable relationships since they are easier to understand intuitively. The argument is applicable, however, to multivariate relationships in which the dependent variable is measured as a deviation from its regression on a set of independent variables already considered.

The classical situation often discussed in this context is one in which the *within-system regressions are the same for all systems and are approximately equal to zero, but the slope of the regression of system means is different from zero.* This is the example of the relationship between being black and being illiterate: there is no relationship within American states, but there is a strong positive relationship at the level of states and even a stronger one at the level of regions. For the sake of illustration we will assume interval measurement at all levels.

Thus, although a person who is black is not more likely to be less literate than a person who is white, states that have a high percentage of blacks also have a high percentage of illiterates.

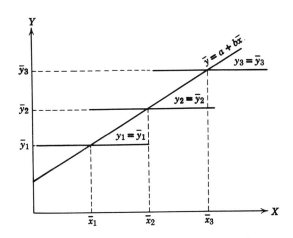

Figure 2

It can be generally shown that whenever within-systems relationships are low, the relationship observed at the level of systems will tend to be larger than the total relationship. This is particularly true in the extreme case when the relationship within systems is zero or nearly zero, as in the example discussed above. A simple mathematical formulation is useful in illustrating this difference. According to the covariance theorem discussed above,[39]

$$r_{XY,t}\, \sigma_{X,t}\, \sigma_{Y,t} = r_{XY,a}\, \sigma_{X,a}\, \sigma_{Y,a} + \sum_{w=1}^{k} r_{XY,w}\, \sigma_{X,w}\, \sigma_{Y,w},$$

where   r is the correlation between two variables,

σ_X, σ_Y are the standard deviations,

t denotes observations made for the total population,

a denotes observations made at the level of groups,

w denotes observations made within groups, and

k is the number of groups.

In other words, the total covariance (left hand of the equation) equals the sum of the among-group and within-group covariances. Thus the among-

[39] See also H. R. Alker, *Mathematics and Politics*, Macmillan, New York, 1965, for a fuller discussion of this theorem.

group covariance equals the difference between the total covariance and the sum of within group covariances:

$$r_{XY,a} \, \sigma_{X,a} \, \sigma_{Y,a} = r_{XY,t} \, \sigma_{X,t} \, \sigma_{Y,t} - \sum_{w=1}^{k} r_{XY,w} \, \sigma_{X,w} \, \sigma_{Y,w}.$$

We are discussing here the situation when the within-group *correlations* are equal to zero (or nearly zero). In this case, the last term equals zero, and

$$r_{XY,a} \, \sigma_{X,a} \, \sigma_{Y,a} = r_{XY,t} \, \sigma_{X,t} \, \sigma_{Y,t}.$$

Therefore,

$$r_{XY,a} = \frac{\sigma_{X,t} \, \sigma_{Y,t}}{\sigma_{X,a} \, \sigma_{Y,a}} r_{XY,t}.$$

But whenever the within-group variances are different from zero, the total variance of a variable will be larger than the variance of system means. Thus the numerator above will be larger than the denominator, and consequently the observed among-group correlation, $r_{XY,\,a}$, will be larger than the true correlation for the entire population, $r_{XY,\,t}$.

When this type of situation is observed, it seems clear that a third variable operates on both variables observed within systems—a variable such as the level of industrialization of a state. In such situations "setting" variables are more likely to provide explanation at the system level than "context" variables. Although this two-variable relationship could be controlled for another individual-level variable, such as family income, the difference between within-system and among-system regressions will remain. The among-system relationship is *spurious* since a system-level variable influences both of the means. In this sense the ecological correlation between the two variables is not "true."

A different situation is encountered when *the among-system correlation equals zero while the within-system correlations are different from zero, or when the within-system regressions* (and according to our assumptions, correlations) *have different sign than the among-system regression.*

For example, imagine that we are studying the relationship between exposure to urban life (years in the city) and attitudes of modernity. In each system the relationship is positive, but the mean of modernity is the same in all countries regardless of the mean of urbanization.

In this situation, *the within-systems regression coefficients, b, are the same,* and the means of the dependent variable are also the same. Thus for two systems the difference between the means of the independent variable, X_w (where $_w$ varies across systems) is a function of the difference between the intercepts of the regressions a_w.

$$\overline{X}_1 - \overline{X}_2 = \frac{a_2 - a_1}{b}$$

Since the intercept, a_w, of the regression line indicates the value of the dependent variable, when the independent variable equals zero it is clear that the difference between within-country and among-country regressions is a result of the differences in *the value of the dependent variable when the independent variable does not operate.* This point may be more easily understood in stochastic terms. In one country the value of the dependent variable, modern attitudes, is higher than in another country before the independent variable, exposure to the city, begins to operate. In one country individuals have "further to go." Although once the independent variable operates, the countries move at the same pace—relationship is the same within all systems—system means of the dependent variable cannot be predicted from the system means of the independent variable. In our example this may mean that before the peasants in one country, say Chile, move to the city, they are more modernity-oriented than, for example, peasants in India.

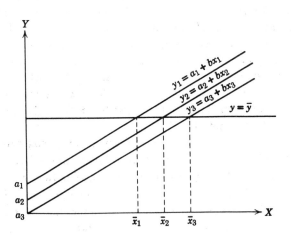

Figure 3

In the example discussed above, the within-system relationships were positive and the among-system relationship (slope and fit) equaled zero. But even more interesting are those situations in which the within- and the among-systems regressions have a different sign. For example, Kornhauser found a highly negative (−.76) rank-order correlation between the proportion of male labor force in nonagricultural occupations and the proportion of votes for the Communist party among fifteen Western countries. He concluded:

"Thus, there is a strong negative relation between the extent to which societies are industrialized and the strength of communism within the Western world. . . ."[40]

This finding is generally used as a refutation of Marx's theory. However, there is ample evidence, as Kornhauser himself shows, not only that workers in larger factories tend to vote Communist, but also, that within each country the extent of industrialization of a certain region or administrative unit is positively related to the Communist vote. Thus there are two seemingly contradictory findings: at the level of countries the relationship between industrialization and Communist vote is negative; within countries it is generally positive. How can these findings be reconciled?

Let us revert again to a diagram. We see that the difference among the means of the dependent variable of each system is a function

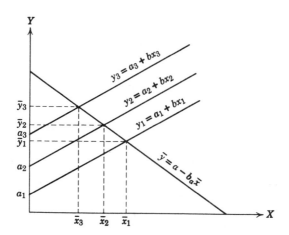

Figure 4

of the regression intercepts. But since the means of the dependent variable are no longer equal from system to system, this difference is also a function of the differences between means of the independent variables. Since, according to regression,

[40] William Kornhauser, *The Politics of Mass Society*, Free Press, Glencoe, Ill., 1959, p. 150.

$$Y_x = a_w + b\overline{X}_x \qquad\qquad Y_w = a_w + bX_w$$

the difference between means of the dependent variable of two systems equals

$$\overline{Y}_i - \overline{Y}_j = (a_i - a_j) - b(\overline{X}_i - \overline{X}_j).$$

It would be outside the scope of this book to discuss formally the general conditions under which the slopes of the within- and the among-systems regressions have different signs. Let us look at a specific case of two systems. Since in the general case we would be seeking the criterion that would permit us to determine when $b_w b_a < 0$, in this specific case one must establish the conditions under which the means of independent and dependent variables of two systems are related differently than the observations within these systems. When the within-systems regressions, assumed thoughout this discussion to be constant, are positive, we are interested in the case in which the difference between the means of the dependent variables has a different sign than the difference between the means of the independent variables. When the slopes of the within-system regressions are negative, it is necessary to find the conditions under which the differences of means have the same signs. In other words, we are interested in the following situation:

and
$$\text{when} \quad b_w > 0, \qquad (\overline{X}_i - \overline{X}_j)\,(\overline{Y}_i - \overline{Y}_j) < 0$$
$$\text{when} \quad b_{ib} < 0, \qquad (\overline{X}_i - \overline{X}_j)\,(\overline{Y}_i - \overline{Y}_j) > 0.$$

Let us assume that these two systems are ordered in such a way that

$$(X_i - X_j) > 0.$$

We can then expect the among-system regression to have a slope signed differently than the within-system regressions if and only if the difference of the intercepts has a sign different from the coefficient of within-system regressions, and the difference between intercepts is larger (in absolute value) than the difference of means multiplied by this regression coefficient. Figure 4 presents the case when the among-system regressions are negative; Figure 5 presents the case when they are positive. The effects of relaxing either of the criteria can be studied by manipulating the slope of regression and the difference between the means of the independent variables.

In the light of this general discussion, Kornhauser's finding must be attributed to the fact that he considered countries that differ relatively little with regard to the independent variable, but differ more with regard to the regression intercepts. As pointed out earlier, regression intercepts indicate the value of the independent variable, in this case Communist vote, when the independent variable, nonagricultural labor force, equals zero. In other

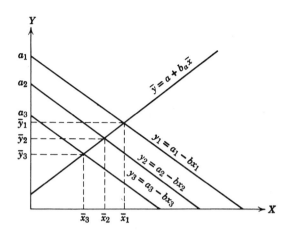

Figure 5

words the ecological correlation observed by Kornhauser is a function of the behavior of persons employed in agriculture, *not outside of it*. What Kornhauser found is that in the most-industrialized countries, *peasants* are less likely to vote Communist, while in the less-industrialized countries they are more likely to do so. Thus what we find is that the process of industrialization brings a progressive differentiation of Communist support between an agricultural and a nonagricultural population—a finding not contrary to Marx's theory. Allardt's finding of the two types of Communism in Finland confirms this prediction of the model analyzed above.[41]

In general, in this situation there is no need to change the level of analysis to system-level variables. The within-system regressions are the same, and the differences in contexts—average modernity of peasants before exposure to city life or their rate of Communist vote in nonindustrialized regions—can be easily adjusted. A difference of initial contexts constitutes the theoretical interpretation of the differences between the within- and among-systems regressions. The system-level or "ecological" interpretation does not merit an independent theoretical interpretation, and is therefore "spurious." But an additional theoretical statement relating the means of the independent variables to regression intercepts can be formulated on the basis of this analysis.

In both of the above situations we concluded that among-system or "ecological" regression does not have a meaningful theoretical interpretation

[41] Erik Allardt, "Patterns of Class Conflict and Working Class Consciousness in Finnish Politics," *op. cit.*

independent of within-system regressions. When regression coefficients within systems equal zero, then differences can be attributed to a system-level variable, most likely of a setting nature, operating at the level of systems. When regression coefficients within systems differed from zero, we concluded that the difference between the within-systems and ecological regressions stems from the differences of the context. In general the ecological relationship is spurious whenever within-system regressions have the same slope, hence on the basis of the assumption of similar variances, the same fit. There is no need to change the level of analysis.

Inferences when Within-System Relationships Differ Systematically

Particularly interesting from the point of view of comparative research are situations in which the *slope of regression lines within each system* is a function of the means of the independent variable in each system. Of several such situations, two will be discussed here.

In the first situation, the within-system observations are well predicted by linear regressions, but the slope of these regressions assumes a different sign within different ranges of the independent variable. An example can

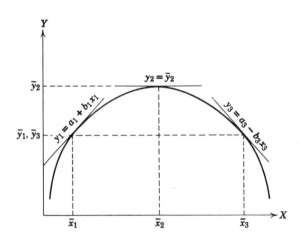

Figure 6

be formulated with countries and regions as levels of analysis. The dependent variable is domestic violence, and the independent variable is the level of economic development. In Africa the level of economic development is low, and the level of violence increases with economic development. In Latin America the level of economic development is higher, and the level of violence is not related to economic development. Finally, in Western Europe, where the level of economic development is high, violence decreases with the increase of the level of economic development.[42] The relationship between means of economic development and violence is curvilinear. Within-system observations fit a linear model only because the range of variation of the independent variable is limited in any particular region. Thus within-system relationships are true only for a limited range of the independent variable, whereas the "true" regression is curvilinear.

A frequent speculation in the social sciences concerns the impact of the social "context" upon the behavior of individuals. Extensive evidence, derived mainly from social psychology, indicates that individuals behave differently when they act alone than when they are members of groups having some specific norms.[43] Assume that a number of groups is available, and within each group a linear prediction fits observations. In other words, within each system the dependent variable linearly depends upon the independent variable. However, if the social context operates, the slope of these linear regression lines differs from system to system in such a way that it either systematically increases or decreases when the group mean for the independent variable increases. The within-systems regressions are linear; among-system regression is again curvilinear and this time monotonic.

Allardt and Pesonen report, for example, that the relationship between the proportion of Swedish-speaking people and the vote for the Swedish party among the Finnish communes increases as the proportion of Swedes increases.[44] If the proportion of Swedes is low in a commune—the system in this analysis—then being a Swede is not associated with a greater likelihood of voting for the Swedish party. If, however, the proportion of Swedes is high, they are much more likely to behave as Swedes, that is, vote for this party. *This is a context effect, whereby the context operates in an interactive manner.*[45] The probability of behaving in a certain way depends upon the proportion of the individuals of a given class within each system. Again, stochastic language may be helpful in elucidating this kind of an effect.

[42] Actually, what we know is that the correlation between a nonmonetary index of economic development and domestic violence is positive (.33) among the underdeveloped countries and negative (−.68) among the developed countries. See H. R. Alker in B. M. Russett *et al., World Handbook of Social and Political Indicators.* Yale University Press, New Haven, Conn., 1964.

[43] For a summary of this evidence see E. L. Walker and R. W. Heyns, *Anatomy of Conformity,* Prentice-Hall, Englewood Cliffs, N.J., 1962.

[44] Allardt and Pesonen, *op. cit.*

[45] This is a generalization of a model constructed by professor Raymond Boudon to explain the Communist vote in France. We thank Professor Boudon for several discussions about this class of models.

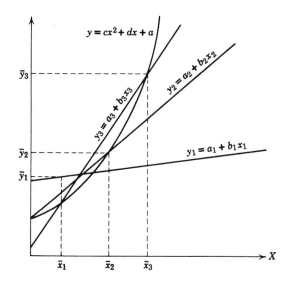

Figure 7

Coleman, et al., discovered that the rate of diffusion of innovation among persons isolated from their social environment does not depend upon the number of persons who have already accepted this innovation. If, however, these persons are integrated into their social context, the rate of adoption does depend upon the level of acceptance at a previous time.[46] In these terms, the stooges in Asch's conformity experiment can be viewed as a social context. The probability of the kth person behaving in a certain way is a function of the $(k - 1)$ number of persons who have behaved this way previously.

The difference of the form between the linear within-system regressions and the nonlinear among-system regression can be explained with a simple model. There are several groups, administrative units, regions, or countries. We are interested in a behavior of the individuals within these systems, for example, the proportion of the vote for a given party—Swedish party in Finland, Communist party in France, Democratic party in the United States. This proportion is explained in terms of the behavior of a particular subgroup within the population of these systems—Swedes in the Finnish communes, workers in the French *départements,* or ethnic population in the American states. In the simplest form, a model without context would express the proportion of the vote for a given party as a sum of the vote of

[46] Reported in J. S. Coleman, *Introduction to Mathematical Sociology,* Free Press, New York, 1964.

groups other than those considered (assumed here to be constant only for the sake of simplicity) and of the size of the relevant group multiplied by its propensity to vote for a given party:

$$Y_i = a + bX_i,$$

where Y_i is the proportion of the vote for the party in system i, a is the proportion of this vote contributed by persons other than those under consideration, constant across systems, X_i is the proportion of the persons under consideration in system i, and b is the propensity of these persons to vote for the given party, constant across systems.

To use a specific example, let the party be the Swedish party in Finland. Then a is the proportion of the vote for the Swedish party contributed by non-Swedes, X_i is the proportion of Swedes in a commune, b is the propensity of the Swedes to vote for the Swedish party. At this moment, this propensity is considered to be constant throughout Finland: in all communes the probability of a Swede voting for the Swedish party is the same.

How can the context be introduced into this model? If the context within which the Swedes vote is an element of the explanation, the propensity to vote for the Swedish party cannot be constant but must depend in turn upon the proportion of Swedes in each community. Thus, instead of a constant b, we have

$$b_i = d + cX_i,$$

where b_i is the propensity of a Swede to vote for the Swedish party in system i, d is that part of their propensity that does not depend upon the presence of other Swedes, c is the "coefficient of context," and X_i is again the proportion of Swedes in system i.

Substituting the new values of b_i's into the original equation, we have

$$Y_i = cX_i^2 + dX_i + a,$$

where Y_i is the proportion of persons who behaved in a given way in system i, X_i is the proportion of persons under consideration in the population of system i, c is the coefficient of context, which indicates the importance of social context in bringing about behavior Y, d is the propensity of the individuals of this group to behave in the specified way, regardless of the social context, and a is the contribution of persons other than those whose behavior is used to explain Y.

It is apparent that the function generated by the equation of the context model is curvilinear in the manner portrayed in Figure 7. Thus when the slopes of linear within-systems regressions change systematically with the mean of the independent variable and, hence, the among-system or "ecological" regression is curvilinear, one may expect that the social context influences the behavior under consideration. In this situation, both the within-system and the among-system regressions require independent theoretical interpretation in terms of the coefficients d and c, defined *above*. Neither relationship is spurious, and no "ecological fallacies" are impending. Two theoretical statements are necessary to explain individual behavior: one that states that an individual behaves in the way Y with probability d when he is an isolated member of group X, and another that states that this probability is increased by c when the social context operates. A system-level variable—the context of individual behavior—must be introduced into the analysis.

Conclusion

We have distinguished above some simplified situations that can be used as analytical models in interpreting the operation of system-level variables on within-system relationships. What is necessary now, even if only in an introductory manner, is to (1) distinguish between "spurious" and "true" correlations when relationships are observed at different levels of analysis and (2) distinguish the effects of the variables observable only at the level of systems (diffusion patterns and settings) from the variables aggregated from within-system observations (contexts).

The currently available theoretical and statistical techniques allow us to distinguish spurious correlations between two variables, X and Y, measured as deviations from their respective regressions on a third variable Z, only when Z is measured at the same level as X and Y. If an assumption can be made concerning the direction of influence, a prediction that the correlation between two variables measured as deviations from their regressions on a third variable is zero can be tested against a set of data. What we need in comparative research, however, are statistical techniques that would allow the control variable to be measured at a level different from the two variables that are tested. The situations discussed above cast only partial light on the problem of interlevel spuriousness. The following criteria can be introduced:

1. If the within-system regressions are the same in all systems and the total regression is also the same, then the relationship between the variables X and Y may at the most be spurious at the individual level. Since our goal is to develop general theories, it seems useful to identify as spurious only within-system relationships that change uniformly (most often disappear) in all systems when a third within-system variable is introduced. Thus when the introduction of a third variable changes the relationship between two

variables only in some systems, the gain of prediction does not justify the loss of generality.

2. If within-system regressions do not differ from zero in all systems, but the total regression does differ from zero, the ecological correlation is spurious. In other words the relationship between X and Y (race and illiteracy) is "true" at the individual level and "spurious" at the system level. Controlling a relationship between the system means for a system-level variable would reduce the among-system relationship to zero—the true value observed at the individual level.

3. If within-system regressions are the same and differ from zero in all systems but the total regression does not differ from zero, the ecological correlation is spurious. An adjustment of the values of the intercepts of within-system regressions would again adjust the among-system regression so that its slope would be the same as the within-system regressions.

4. If the regression coefficients differ from system to system, the among-system regression is equally true as the within-system regressions, since both regressions require theoretical interpretation. These interpretations depend upon the nature of the factors operating at the level of systems.

We have assumed in this discussion that *within-system* relationships are linear or, in other words, that there are no interaction effects *at the individual level*. The relationship between education and achievement motivation, for example, was assumed to be independent of the level of education, that is, an increase in achievement motivation associated with an increase of education is constant. This assumption is often unwarranted. Interactions may occur in all or in some systems. But the discussion of individual-level interactions would exceed the limits of the present problem.

We argued in the introduction to this chapter that whenever the within-system relationships are not the same, the analysis should be shifted to the level of systems. Subsequently an additional criterion was introduced consisting of the difference between the within-system regressions and the regression among means. In light of the discussion, however, the original criterion does not require modification because whenever relationships within systems are the same the relationship among means differing from the within-system relationships is considered spurious.

CHAPTER FOUR

Formulating Theories Across Systems

Introduction: A Restatement. Formulating General Statements.
Comparative Explanation in the Social Sciences: A Conclusion.

Introduction: A Restatement

The role of theory in the social sciences and some of the assumptions and implications of the accepted model of theory in the context of comparative research have been discussed in the preceding chapters. In this chapter we shall construct a procedure for formulating general statements. In order to set the context within which this procedure is justified some of the definitions and assumptions will be restated.

"Comparative" studies were defined as those in which the influence of larger systems upon the characteristics of units within them is examined at some stage of analysis. Consequently comparative studies involve at least two levels of analysis. In this sense not all of the studies conducted across systems or nations are comparative, but all studies that are comparative are cross-systemic. If national social, political, or economic systems constitute one of the levels of analysis, the study is a cross-national comparative study. If, however, the anlysis is conducted exclusively at the level of nations, then according to this definition it is not comparative.

A theory explains and predicts social phenomena. The explanations should be accurate, general, parsimonious, and causal. The implications of this role of theory for comparative studies are the following: (1) General theoretical statements, valid regardless of the social systems involved, should be sought. (2) Whenever they can be assessed validly across systems, general concepts should be used. (3) Whenever necessary, the influence of system-level factors on a class of phenomena should be incorporated into the explanation. General statements can be formulated across systems if within-system relationships do not differ—if systems do not contribute to explanation. Whenever systems differ, some factor operating at the system level is influencing the within-systems relationships.

To illustrate the logic of this argument, let us return to M. Rouget, the French worker, age 24, employed in a large factory. He votes for a party of the Left, and we want to understand why. We explained his behavior in terms of some general statements found to be true of Frenchmen. But if several studies have confirmed that in all systems in which the option of voting for the Left is present, young workers employed in large factories are likely to vote for a leftist party with the probability of .60 to .70, the vote of M. Rouget can now be explained in exactly the same way as the behavior of Senor Martinez, a Chilean, or of a young worker in Norway. Regardless of the social system in which the behavior of individuals occur, the same theory is valid: young workers employed in large factories tend to vote Communist. But if an additional explanatory factor is considered, this theory is no longer equally true. When the sex of a French or a Chilean worker is considered, the explanation of the vote becomes more complete. Males in France and Chile are more likely to vote Communist than females. The introduction of this explanatory factor increases the probability of the Communist vote of young workers employed in large factories to .80. But in Norway voting for the Left is independent of sex. At this stage the explanation must include a statement of the relevant characteristics of France and Chile, on the one hand, and Norway, on the other. If this explanation is to be theoretical, then it is not sufficient to state that "in France males vote Left more often than females, while in Norway there are no differences between sexes in voting."

An explanatory statement must be logically open to extension to other cases. Instead of specifying the names of social systems, therefore, a variable operating at the level of systems must be added to the explanation. For example, it may be that wherever the role of established religious organizations is strong, there will be a difference in the voting behavior of men and women. The explanation of the vote of M. Rouget would then assume the following form:

1. M. Rouget is a young male worker employed in a large factory *in a social system* in which the church plays an important role, and

2. young workers employed in large factories tend to vote Left with the probability of .60 to .70, and in those systems in which the role of

church is strong, men vote Left more often than women; *therefore, it is highly likely* (probability of .80) that

   3. M. Rouget votes for a party of the Left.

The premises of the explanation of the vote of Mr. Janson, a Norwegian, *would be the same,* but the second premise concerning the systemic conditions under which the behavior of men differs from that of women, would not provide any gain in prediction. Thus the behavior of both individuals, a Frenchman and a Norwegian, would be explained in terms of the same theory, but the explanation of the behavior of a Frenchman would be more complete—the probability that the conclusion is true would be higher.

An explanation of a specific property of an individual or a social unit calls for a confirmed general statement pertaining to this class of properties. In this sense accumulation of knowledge is a sequence of confirmations and/or modifications of theories. Theory-building and theory-testing are aspects of the same process. Theories not tested by any reference to empirical evidence have a zero degree of confirmation.[1] As predictions drawn from a theory are tested against observable instances, the theory gains confirmation. If the predictions do not hold, a theory may be modified or even rejected. Theories are not falsified by specific tests of the derivable hypotheses, however, but as a result of their overall usefulness for predicting a given class of events. The process of confirming and/or modifying theories will be referred to as the "formulation" of theories. The formulation of théories is conceived of as an interplay between constructing and modifying deductive systems and testing hypotheses through empirical research. This concept has an advantage over the more familiar concepts of theory-building and theory-testing since it avoids connotations of an inductive approach to theory-building and does not equate tests of specific hypotheses with evaluations of general theories.

Formulating Comparative Theories: A Procedure

Let us denote all factors analyzed within systems as either D (a dependent variable) or I_i (independent variables), where i varies from 1 to k. Let us denote the factors operating at the level of systems as S_i, where i varies from $k + 1$ to p. Finally, let us define the error of prediction, the

---

[1] For the concept of confirmation see C. G. Hempel, *Aspects of Scientific Explanation and Other Essays in the Philosophy of Science,* Free Press, New York, 1965, particularly the essay on "Confirmation, Induction, and Rational Belief," pp. 1–81 and pp. 381–94; and Rudolf Carnap, "The Aim of Inductive Logic," in E. Nagel, P. Suppes, and A. Tarski, eds., *Logic Methodology, and Philosophy of Science,* Stanford University Press, Stanford, Calif., 1962.

unexplained part of variation of the dependent phenomenon, as N^*, where i varies across the social systems, from 1 to n, and indicates the degree of completeness of explanation in each system. We shall assume that there are no systematic errors operating at the level of systems. The dependent variable, D, will be a function of the two sets of independent variables, defined above.

$$D = f(I_i, S_i) + N^*.$$

The form of this function is defined by a particular theory.

If measurement is free of error, that part of the variation of the dependent variable unexplained by the theory can be treated as a function of the factors that influence the dependent phenomenon but *have not been included* in the theory. Let us denote this set of factors relative to each social system as N_j (without the asterisk). Then the error of prediction is a function of variables not included in the theory:

$$N^*_j = f(N_j).$$

The dependent variable can now be defined as a function of three sets of variables:[2]

$$D = f(I_i, S_i, N_j).$$

Prior to any explanation, when the dependent variable is only measured within each system, the residual error, N^*_j, is the same as the total variation. In other words, all of the independent variables are at this moment subsumed under the names of systems.

$$N_j = (I_i, S_i); \qquad i = 1, 2, \ldots, p.$$

The procedure is, *first*, to find determinants of the dependent variable that account for its variance without reference to any systemic factors and, *second*, to develop explanation with system-level factors. This procedure can be thought of in terms of a multivariate statistical technique that partials the variance of the dependent variable: stepwise multiple regression applied "simultaneously" to different systems; an interaction detector technique analyzing the relative importance of different predictors; or analysis of variance comparing the influence of within-system classifications to classifications based on systems. Which of these approaches is most suitable is a matter of the nature of the data under consideration.

The logic described above best conforms to a stepwise multiple regression conducted separately within each system and with intersystem comparisons

---

[2] This was suggested in a somewhat less detailed form by Johan Galtung in "Some Aspects of Comparative Research," *Polls*, 2, 1965.

at each step. 1. The first step in comparative research is the definition and measurement of a dependent variable, D. Let us assume we are formulating a theory of political participation and the dependent variable is "mobilization into politics," defined as psychological and behavioral "membership" in the political system.[3] Political mobilization is measured through various indicators of political awareness and participation, such as knowledge of the political system, interest in politics, voting, membership in a political organization, and attendance at political meetings. Let us assume that we have obtained sets of interval-scale scores of political mobilization describing random samples of individuals within several countries.

The first question is whether systems, in this case nations, are the "same" or "different" on the dependent variable. As was emphasized earlier, if nations do not differ on the dependent variable, the problem of explanation is not a comparative one. System-level factors do not operate on the dependent variable, and therefore explanation can remain at the individual level. All observations can be treated as if they were derived from the same population. In this situation the explanation of the dependent variable can proceed as if it were a one-system study: the samples of respondents can be pooled, and political mobilization can be related to other variables common to and measurable within all countries. We may later discover that a multivariate relationship is curvilinear, and we may then examine whether this curvilinearity does not coalesce with the systems.

Various sets of data will indicate the extent of political mobilization in several countries. For example, if party identification is used as an indicator, we would find that mobilization is high in the United States and Germany (above 70 percent),[4] somewhat lower in Japan (62 percent),[5] and even lower in France (45 percent).[6] Since the available information is highly scattered and derived from different sources, however, this information should be treated merely as an illustration of intersystemic differences. Further discussion will concern only such cases in which the existence of intersystemic differences is assumed.

---

[3] The concept of political mobilization used here was defined in Krzysztof Ostrowski and Adam Przeworski, "A Preliminary Inquiry into the Nature of Social Change: the Case of the Polish Countryside," *International Journal of Comparative Sociology,* **8,** 1967.

[4] Data for the United States are from P. E. Converse and Georges Dupeux, "Politicization of the Electorate in France and in the United States," in L. A. Coser, ed., *Political Sociology,* Harper & Row, New York, 1966, and from A. J. Heidenheimer, *The Governments of Germany,* Crowell, New York, 1966. Data for Germany are from Heidenheimer, *ibid.*

[5] *Polls,* **1,** 1966.

[6] Converse and Dupeux, *op. cit.*

2. If there is a cross-system difference, the question is what are the factors that influence the dependent variable—why did the difference occur? The presence of a difference, however, is treated, merely as an indication that the problem is comparative.

The question that must be answered is whether a within-system variable, I_1, explains the dependent variable, D, in all of the systems. Formally the test is whether the fit of prediction is more or less the same for all systems. We are testing a hypothesis that the correlation between the dependent variable and the first-selected independent variable is the same in all systems. If the statistical technique was analysis of variance, we would ask whether the sum of squares accounted for in each social system is the same.

2.1. If the answer is positive—the two variables are positively, negatively, or not at all related in all countries—we can formulate our first theoretical statement. For example, Converse and Dupeux discovered that, although the rates of party identification differ between France and the United States, in both systems the crucial variable explaining this identification is political socialization through the family.[7] To continue our example, let us say that the first statement that holds across systems is that political mobilization is a result of exposure to mass media; in all countries there is a positive correlation between exposure and political mobilization.

Since the independent variable is related in the same way to the dependent variable in all systems, we can apply the procedure that corrects the original scores on the dependent variable. We can ask what the scores on the dependent variable *would have been* if the dependent variable were the same for all countries. The larger the variations of the independent variable and the stronger the relationship, the more the values of the dependent variable will change as a result of this adjustment.

2.2. Let us suppose that the correlations do differ among systems. For example, in some countries persons who own radios are more likely to be politically mobilized than those who do not, while in another group of countries this relationship is negligible. An additional question can now be asked. It can be formulated in two ways.

2.2.1. If one finds that the relationship between political mobilization and the exposure to radio is positive in one country and negligible in another, it is possible to ask whether there is another variable in the latter country that is related to the same dependent variable and can be considered as belonging to the domain of the *same general* concept. Let us say, for example, that in the country where the original correlation

[7] Converse and Dupeux, *op. cit.*

was negligible, exposure to television is related to political mobilization. The theory can now be modified: instead of talking about "exposure to radio" and "exposure to television," we can treat both of them as specific instances of a more general concept, "exposure to mass media." The new, more general statement will now say that "political mobilization is related to exposure to mass media, wherein ownership of radio and television sets indicate exposure to mass media." This kind of statement must be based on an explicit model of measurement that allows this kind of operation on uncorrelated indicators. In this case the level of generality of the concept will be shifted upward, and a statement analogous to one saying that relationships are the same for all systems (2.1.) can be made.

2.2.2. An alternative question can be posed in terms of controlling for some other variable rather than of increasing the generality of variables. Instead of asking whether there are indicators in the two systems that can be generalized into an index correlated with the dependent variable, one can ask whether there is a common variable that, if controlled, modifies the original correlation so it becomes the same in all countries. Let us assume that urbanization is such a variable in two countries under study. In the first country political mobilization is related to farm size, and in the second country it is not. But in the first country, urbanization is correlated with both variables; in the second country urbanization influences the size of a farm, but not political mobilization, the dependent variable. A diagram will best portray this example:

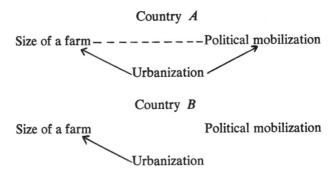

Country *A*

Size of a farm — — — — — — — — — —Political mobilization

Urbanization

Country *B*

Size of a farm   Political mobilization

Urbanization

The relationship between the dependent variable and the first considered independent variable is spurious in the first country since both of these phenomena in turn depend (share most of their covariance) upon urbanization. When urbanization is controlled, the relationship is negligible in both countries. In other cases, controlling for a third variable may bring out a relationship between two variables in the country in which it was not initially present.

2.3. We have found that the first independent variable is related in the same way to the dependent variable in all countries. In some cases, this relationship became the same only when either specific variables were generalized to a new concept or a common variable was controlled in all systems. The first theoretical statement can now be formulated. This statement will describe the dependent variable as a function of one independent variable and residual factors.

$$D = f(I_1, N_j),$$

where

$$N_i' = N_j - (I_1).$$

If a difference of relationships cannot be removed either by a reformulation of the independent variable or by controlling for a third variable, however, this independent variable, I_1, *will not enter the theory at this time.* The search should continue until another variable is discovered that does provide a uniform explanation in all systems.

3. Having identified one common explanatory variable, we can now repeat the testing operations. This repetition will involve all steps described under 2., plus some new procedures. The question is whether another independent variable contributes to the explanation of the dependent phenomenon after the one variable has been accepted, that is, after the variance of the dependent variable is reduced in each system by the part that is accounted for by the first variable. For example, if exposure to mass media was found to explain political mobilization in all systems, the question could be asked whether the degree of education further contributes to the explanation of political mobilization. The hypothesis to be tested is that the relationship between the second independent variable, I_2, and the dependent variable, D, is the same in all systems *and* that I_2 contributes more to the explanation of political mobilization than exposure to mass media alone. First, we ask whether the new variable, I_2, education, is related in the same way to the dependent variable, political mobilization, in all systems.

3.1. If the answer is negative, we must ask whether there are any more variables (or degrees of freedom) available. If the answer is positive, we can retrace the steps described under 3. and continue testing until either the number of variables or degrees of freedom is exhausted. *Whenever there are no more variables that provide a similar explanation regardless of the social systems, the level of analysis must be changed to S variables.* This change is described under 5.

3.2. Now the answer is positive: the new variable is related to D in the same way in all systems. The first part of the test—uniformity of relationships—has been satisfied. In order to establish that I_2 contributes something new to the explanation of D, it must be shown that I_2 is *not* related in the same way to the first independent variable, I_1, *whenever this relationship is different from zero.* In other words, if I_2 together with I_1 is to account for more variance of D than I_1 alone, then I_2 must be correlated with D, but not with I_1. Education can provide an *independent* explanation of political mobilization if and only if it explains a different part of political mobilization than does exposure to mass media—education and mass media must be unrelated.

3.3. If I_2 and D are related positively or negatively in all systems and I_2 is related to I_1 in all countries, then one of the correlations—$r_{I_1 D}$ or $r_{I_2 D}$—can be considered as spurious. When education is related both to exposure to mass media and to political mobilization, the relationship between exposure to mass media and mobilization is "spurious": the degree of education constitutes an explanation of both the exposure and the mobilization. If an individual is educated, he is both exposed to mass media and politically mobilized. In this case our original statement, according to which

$$D = f(I_1, N_j'),$$

must be replaced by the statement that

$$D = f(I_1, I_2, N_j''),$$

which can be read as "whenever I_2 is considered, it replaces I_1 as a predictor of D."

3.4. If the second independent variable contributes *independently* to the explanation of the dependent phenomenon, the inclusion of I_2 will increase the proportion of the variance of D explained by the theory. Let us now say that I_1 and I_2 have either an *independent* or an *interactive* effect on D—an effect that is larger than that of either I_1 or I_2 alone. For example, if an individual is exposed to mass media *and* is a member of nonpolitical organizations, he is very likely to be mobilized politically. The dependent variable is a function of two independent variables and the national residuum:

$$D = f(I_1, I_2, N''_j),$$

where

$$N''_j = N_j - (I_1, I_2).$$

4. Regardless whether the first variable, I_1, or the second one, I_2, or both, contribute to the explanation of the dependent phenomenon, testing

can continue until there are either no more variables or no more degrees of freedom left. The same operation, gradually growing in complexity, must be repeated. If the addition of new independent variables continues to bring explanations that do not differ from country to country, the test is positive and can be continued. When no more variables are available, the level of analysis must be shifted. The two-step description of the test of independent contribution to the explanation of the dependent phenomenon is discussed here for the sake of logical rather than technical clarity. Most multivariate techniques provide both tests simultaneously by showing the increases in the variance of the dependent variable accounted for with the addition of each new variable, and the partial correlations between the ith independent variable and the dependent variable when $(i - 1)$ variables are controlled for.

The statements resulting from these operations express the dependent variable as a function of the independent variables that are measurable within all systems and that provide a uniform explanation regardless of the systems. These statements will provide the most parsimonious and general explanation. In our example, we have formulated the following explanatory statements; political mobilization depends upon exposure to mass media and membership in nonpolitical organizations. This general form of explanation uniform across systems is the following:

$$D = f(I_1, I_2, \ldots, I_k, N_j^k),$$

where

$$N_j^k = N_j - (I_1, I_2, \ldots, I_k).$$

5. Since all the variables that in all systems are related in the same way to the dependent variable have been considered, we now face situations in which the relationship between an additional independent variable and the dependent phenomenon varies from system to system. Let us use as an example the influence of involvement in the market on political mobilization. In one group of countries this relationship is positive and in another negligible. The question is what system-level variables or characteristics are associated with the differences of relationships between market involvement and political mobilization.

System-level variables most closely associated with the within-system correlations would enter into the explanation of the dependent phenomenon. For example, suppose that the relationship between market involvement and political mobilization is high wherever the market is free, that is, wherever the government does not regulate prices. The nature of the market will then become the system-level variable explaining political mobilization. The general statement will now have the following form:

$$D = f(I_1, I_2, \ldots, S_{k+1} \cdot I_3, N_j'''').$$

This statement can be read as "the dependent phenomenon, D, depends upon I_1 and I_2 regardless of systems and upon I_3, depending upon the systemic characteristic S_1." In our example, we can say that political mobilization depends upon exposure to mass media and urbanization regardless of the system involved, and in the systems that have a free market it also depends upon the extent of market involvement. A system-level variable need not be dichotomous: for example, the relationships between exposure to mass media and political mobilization may be a function of the level of economic development of a country.

The procedure of shifting the level of analysis to system variables and formulating explanatory statements relative to systemic characteristics can be repeated until either the number of variables or degrees of freedom is exhausted. We may find that among those countries that have a free market and, thus, where political mobilization depends upon market involvement, the relationship between political mobilization and income in turn depends upon the competitiveness of the party system. If a party system is competitive, persons with high incomes are more likely to be politically mobilized than persons with lower incomes. If, however, a party system is not competitive, personal income does not contribute to the explanation of political mobilization.

Since the number of systems is often limited, the number of degrees of freedom will be exhausted almost immediately. Thus most system-level explanations will be overdetermined: *several system-level variables will equally well account for the same differences of within-system relationships.* Which of these variables "causes" the dependent phenomenon will not be known. This is the point at which social science practice sharply departs from the model of theory. At some stage in the formation of theory, we will be forced to state that "*in all systems,* political mobilization depends upon I_1 and I_2; *in systems with high S_1,* it depends upon I_3; *in systems with low S_1,* it depends upon I_4; *in systems with low S_1 and high S_2,* it depends upon I_5, but *in Poland* it also depends upon I_6." At this point the proper name of the social system will be introduced. The name still serves to identify the residual factors that have not been isolated. The incompleteness of explanation or the error, $N*_j$, depends upon the factors subsumed under the name of the social system. Thus the "unique" features of a nation, as they are traditionally termed, should be considered broadly as including not only phenomena that do not have counterparts in other countries—*liberum veto* in Poland or the "melting pot" in the United States—but also all other characteristics of a nation that were not isolated in the process of formulating a theory. An example of a theory concerning political mobilization is presented below.

Theory of Political Mobilization, All Systems

"Political mobilization depends upon exposure to mass
media, membership in nonpolitical organizations,
and political socialization through the family."

Systems with a Free Market
"Residual political mobilization
depends upon market involvement."

Systems with a Regulated Market
"Residual political mobilization
depends upon intergenerational
mobility."

*Systems with
Competitive
Parties*
"Residual political mobilization
depends upon individual income."

*Systems without
Competitive
Parties*

India
"Residual
political
mobilization
depends upon
size of the
community."

Chile
"Residual
political
mobilization
depends upon
religiosity."

Theory: Political mobilization depends upon exposure to mass media, membership in nonpolitical organizations, and political socialization through the family; in those systems that have a regulated market, political mobilization depends upon individual mobility; in systems with free markets, political mobilization depends upon market involvement; if parties compete, it depends upon individual income; in addition, in India it depends upon size of the community and in Chile, upon religiosity.

The theory in the illustration is certainly not very general and its deductive structure is almost nonexistent, but it is an example of a "middle-range" theory particularly frequent in political science. In a more general and deductively more powerful version, one might attempt to formulate a theory in terms of reinforcement learning and structural patterns of rewards and sanctions. Such a theory would state that in all systems individuals enter politics if they have learned that political participation is rewarded. In systems with a free market these rewards are mainly economic, whereas in systems in which the market is regulated the rewards are status and political power. The theory presented in the diagram would then be deductible from a general theory of learning, with systemic characteristics defining patterns of rewards.

Comparative Explanation in the Social Sciences: A Conclusion

This systematic exposition of the steps involved in the comparative confirmation and/or modification of theories closes the discussion of the role of comparative studies in the formulation of social science theories. The main role of a theory is to provide explanations of specific events. These explanations consist of inferring, with a high degree of probability, statements about particular events from general statements concerning classes of events. The procedure for formulating such statements places emphasis on finding explanations that are valid across all social systems and on replacing names of social systems with system-level variables. It is easier to formulate theories that are parsimonious than those that are causal and general. But as knowledge accumulates, the invariance of particular explanatory statements will become known and theories will become more "causal." The gradual increase in the generality of theories seems to be a concomitant of the development of a science.

This interpretation of the nature of theory and the role of comparative social research in the formulation of theories is intended to apply to all social science disciplines. Although the phenomena under consideration vary from discipline to discipline, the logic of scientific inquiry is the same for all social sciences. As the theories explaining social events become general, the explanations of particular events will cut across presently accepted borders of particular disciplines. Some political phenomena may be best explained in terms of learning and, in turn, the explanation of personality characteristics may require societal factors.[8] The explanation of historical events, in spite of their alleged "uniqueness," is not an exception to this interpretation. General laws are necessary in order to explain properties of any event.

As has been stated, the most serious challenge to this interpretation arises from the alleged idiographic nature of historical events. All events are unique. But this does not imply that their explanation cannot be based on general theories. Unless uniqueness is seen in a highly literal sense in which every property of an event is in a class by itself, even unique events do not defy theoretical explanation. What is unique about Catherine II writing letters to Voltaire or Napoleon attacking Russia? Even though the combination of specific circumstances that accompanied the particular act of an individual might have been unrepeated, each of

---

[8] An interesting example showing the influence of nationality, religion, and socioeconomic status on propensity toward conflict and interpersonal emphasis of children can be found in K. W. Terhune, "An Examination of Some Contributing Demographic Variables in a Cross-National Study." *The Journal of Social Psychology,* **59,** 1963.

the properties of these circumstances constitutes an element of a class of such properties. Thus theories formulated in terms of classes of properties will provide an explanation of an event that was never repeated in its entirety. It would be nonsensical to believe that no other person behaved like Catherine II or Napoleon, or that there was only one cosmopolitan elite. Unique events manifest properties of general classes and can be explained by general statements, even if incompletely.

What is needed is systematic accumulation of knowledge about social reality—confirmation and/or modification of the same theories under broadly varying sets of social circumstances. What is needed is comparative research guided by explicit theories and replicating tests of the same general propositions.

PART TWO
Measurement

CHAPTER FIVE

Measurement in Comparative Research

The Language of Comparison. Direct versus Inferred Measurement.
Direct Measurement in Comparative Research. Inferred Measurement:
System Validity and System Interference. Equivalent Measurement
Across Systems. Summary and Conclusions.

Everyday language contains an implicit comparative structure. To say that the economy of the United States is "competitive" implies that the United States can be differentiated from other countries on the basis of this property, or at least that it is possible for a country not to have a competitive economy. In social science, comparative descriptive statements are made with increasing frequency, if not increasing care. Both populations and systems are subject to comparison. Contrasting the scores of samples of national populations is a more systematic form of the previous, more general characterizations of these populations found in the literature on national character. Characterizations of social or political systems are less disciplined by the rudiments of scientific method than are those of national populations whose sampling criteria are available. Argumentative and authoritative criteria prevail in assessing the "authoritarian," "totalitarian," "democratic," "traditional," "modern," or "underdeveloped" properties of social and political systems.

These comparisons generally proceed without an explicit language of comparison. As a result the discussions of specific comparisons are enclosed within a vague set of criteria named as the "same," "identical," "similar," "parallel," "equivalent," and "having a common core." Scientific languages, however, must be explicit. One such language is the language of measurement. This language can be used as a metalanguage of comparison. But the question is what adjustments should be made in the language of measurement in order to meet the persistent problems of measurement that have been identified in comparative research? Problems of measurement arise in comparative research largely from the need to incorporate contextual characteristics of complex systems into the language of measurement.

The problem discussed in this chapter is whether a language of scientific measurement, necessary for formulating theories, can incorporate the context of specific systems, and if so, how the social context can be introduced into measurement statements without destroying the uniformity and generality of the language of measurement.

The Language of Comparison

In the formulation of theory the prescription should be similarity or universality. This prescription is derived from the epistemological justifications of scientific inquiry. The prescription in measurement, however, should be that of dissimilarity. This prescription is derived from the phenomenological foundation of science. Whereas science is general and quantitative in its conclusions, it is specific and qualitative in its observations.

Social scientists make their observations in specific social systems. These observations are either coded directly into a language with direct rules of interpretation, such as "this is a demonstration," or placed indirectly into a language on the basis of inferential rules, such as "in this system demonstrations are a form of social protest." The use of inferential rules is beset with difficulties that are often seen as peculiar to comparative measurement.

The argument against the use of general inferential rules in comparative measurement is that the only appropriate framework for assessing characteristics of social phenomena must be derived from the systems in which observations are made. Morris-Jones states that in the Western idiom certain forms of Indian political behavior are clearly corrupt, whereas in the idiom of the Indian political system, the same behavior is an expression of loyalty.[1] These arguments must be taken seriously. For specific observations, a belch is a belch and nepotism is nepotism. But within an inferential framework a belch is an "insult" or a "compliment" and nepotism is "corruption" or "responsibility." A language of direct measurement requires only a grammar and rules of empirical interpretation invariant across cultures or societies. A language of inferential measurement requires, additionally, general statements defining the meaning of a specific observation in terms of its systemic context.

[1] W. H. Morris-Jones, *The Government and Politics of India,* Doubleday, New York, 1964.

Whether two or more phenomena are "comparable" depends on whether their properties have been expressed in a standard language. A language of measurement defines classes of phenomena by providing specific criteria for deciding whether an observation can be assigned to a particular class. It also orders relationships among those classes.[2] It is a standard language if it can be consistently applied to all individuals or social units. In order to compare the modernity of an Indian peasant and an American business-man, they must both be assigned some of the terms of a standard language. Classifying observations into categories, ranking them, or counting in-stances serves to express observations in a language of measurement. To classify the political system of one country as democratic and another as totalitarian, to order countries in terms of the extent of their political development, or to count the number of persons participating in formal elections is to measure a property of the political system. If these obser-vations are expressed in a standard language, they are indeed comparable. The metalanguage for determining comparability is the language of meas-urement.

Certain criteria of comparability become available as a result of this interpretation of measurement in comparative research. First, the language in which the observations are expressed must contain rules of empirical interpretation. It must be uniformly applicable to all observations. This language must, second, specify the classes or magnitudes that can be assigned to observations. Finally, the relationships among classes, and hence the admissible tranformations, must be stated. If these criteria are met, then it is possible to say that more Indians agree with a question than Americans or that voting turnout is lower in the United States than in Norway.

A language of measurement expressing relationships among classes of objects involves a choice of a model of measurement. Any language is indifferent to the reality to which it is applied. A language of ranking can be applied to a hierarchy of social classes as well as of angels. In the latter case, the classes of this language would be empirically empty. The question of similarity or isomorphism of a language to the phenomena observed is often an open question. Rules of empirical interpretation should be sufficiently explicit so that the process of assigning observations to categories is unambiguous. Measurement statements should be stable across different observations of the same phenomena within the same language.

[2] The literature on the logic of measurement is extensive. Although many issues remain open, we have adhered to standard interpretations. See, for example, Patrick Suppes and J. L. Zinnes, "Basic Measurement Theory," in R. D. Luce, R. R. Bush, and E. Galanter, eds., *Handbook of Mathematical Psychology*, John Wiley & Sons, New York, 1963, pp. 1–76.

The use of a standard language poses no inherent problems for comparative research. Admittedly there will be difficulties in assigning observations to the terms of a formal language, and these difficulties may be greater in one society than in another. The problem of measurement in comparative research arises when the validity of inferential rules is relative to the systems in which the observations are made. At issue is the framework for making inferences regarding deferential behavior from an observation of a person bowing in Egypt. For direct measurement, the problem is that of stable application of the rules of empirical interpretation of a given language. This is the problem of reliability. When inferences are made, however, the problem of reliability is compounded by that of validity. Unless standard rules are available, the cultural or societal contexts in which the observations are made may distort the validity of the inferences.

Direct versus Inferred Measurement

There are two basic procedures whereby observations enter a standard language: one requiring inference and one not. In order for a phenomenon to enter a logical system, a set of operations is necessary. In one case a phenomenon is defined in terms of the operations that are used to measure it. The concept and the procedures of assessment are equated. In survey research, party identification is sometimes defined as a response to the question whether a person considers himself a strong Democrat, a weak Democrat, an Independent, a weak Republican, or a strong Republican.[3] Most concepts used in survey research, especially when responses to particular questions are related to other responses, are measured in this way. This kind of measurement is also frequent in cross-national studies using aggregate data.[4] For example, if the concept is "percent of speakers of the dominant language" and the measuring operation consists of counting the number of people speaking each language, the definition and measurement operation are equated. An operational definition is one in which the level of generality or the "domain" of a concept is coterminous with the result of a measurement operation. Such measurement is direct.

Definitions that are equated with measurement operations can be complex. They are often formed by combining several direct measures. For example, political stability can be defined as a weighted sum of the number of changes of chief executives, number of attempted coups, and the number

[3] See Angus Campbell, P. E. Converse, W. E. Miller, and D. E. Stokes, *The American Voter*, John Wiley & Sons, New York, 1960.

[4] Bruce Russett, et al., *World Handbook of Social and Political Indicators*, Yale University Press, New Haven, Conn., 1964.

of riots. Although such a definition is sometimes referred to as an index, it does not indicate; it defines. The generality of a concept does not extend beyond the results of the *particular* measuring operations.

Since in direct measurement the operations are synonymous with the concept, the results of these operations will necessarily be valid. If political identification is defined as an answer to a particular question, measurement is valid tautologically. Since it is possible that errors have been made in assigning the terms of the language to the observations, however, reliability can be questioned and assessed.

The theoretical significance of concepts defined in terms of specific measuring operations is limited. The generality of such concepts is relatively low and often specific to a social system. A theory of voting will be less general and thus less theoretically significant than a theory of political participation. Voting can be used as a specific phenomenon indicating a level of political participation rather than as a phenomenon that *defines* participation in politics.

Since many concepts of general theoretical significance cannot be defined satisfactorily by a specific measuring operation, inferences are made from the specific observations to general phenomena. Specific phenomena are treated as indicators or pointers. The inferences are based on general laws about behavior. The interdependence of the volume of physical objects and heat can be used in inferential measurement. The volume of mercury under prescribed conditions is used to measure the temperature of the air around it. On the basis of the general psychological law that people who have a certain disposition manifest it verbally, the number of times achievement themes are mentioned is used to make inferences about an individual's achievement motivation.[5] Under the general assumption that effective governments increase social services, the number of hospital beds is the basis for inferring governmental effectiveness.[6]

Generally when measurement is based on inference, the domain of a concept is assumed to be more general than any specific set of indicators actuallly used in measurement. However, if both the phenomenon named by a concept and a phenomenon treated as an indicator can be observed directly, inferences can be made on the basis of this single indicator. For example, social class can be defined by the relative position that an individual holds in his community, expressed as a participant-observation score. The question is then how one can short-cut costly observational operations by the use of simple indicators. Warner found that social class defined in this manner can be predicted on the basis of a few indicators, such as

[5] D. C. McClelland, *The Achieving Society,* D. Van Nostrand, Princeton, N.J., 1961.
[6] S. M. Lipset, *Political Man,* Doubleday, New York, 1960.

education, place of residence, income, and occupation.[7] In some cases these indicators could be further reduced to a single manifestation of class, such as the material used to cover the roof of a residence. The proverbial subject of envy of social scientists is the psychometric test of the "capacity to produce light bulbs," which can be easily validated against actual performance. When both the indicator and the concept can be independently and directly observed, *criterion* validity of the inferences can be established.[8] This kind of measurement is still direct, since inferences used in such measurement are not based on assumptions derived from a theory but inferences simply evaluated in terms of statistical dependence of directly observable phenomena.

A different situation is confronted when the phenomena denoted by a concept cannot be observed directly. It is then necessary to rely on a set of indicators that, it is assumed, *would be related to the phenomenon if it were observed.* "Dispositional properties" are assessed in this manner. Psychological traits such as authoritarianism and systemic characteristics such as integration are assessed on the basis of inferences.

Direct Measurement in Comparative Research

Direct measurement is based on definitions by fiat. Such definitions take the form, "let *S* be the result of observational procedure *X* expressed in this language." For example, "let the level of economic development be per capita national product as recorded in the statistics and expressed in United States dollars." "Aspirations for political power" were defined by Kuroda in his study of Japan and the United States as an answer to the question "would you like to have more (or less) influence?"[9] Although direct observation is the foundation of all measurement, definitions by fiat are limited to such observations. When these observations are stated in a standard language, as defined above, the result is a set of measurement statements allowing comparisons of all cases described in this language.

Direct measurement requires that the language of measurement be common to all observations, reflect relationships among the phenomena

---

[7] W. L. Warner and P. S. Lunt, *The Social Life of a Modern Community,* Yale University Press, New Haven, Conn., 1941.

[8] "Criterion" validity should be distinguished from "construct" validity. Criterion validity is assessed on the basis of the correlation between an observed phenomenon and its indicator. Construct validity is based on the correlation between two sets of indicators of a phenomenon that is not observed directly.

[9] Yasumasa Kuroda, "A Cross-Cultural Analysis of the Desire for Political Power: Empirical Findings and Theoretical Implications," *Western Political Quarterly,* **20,** 1967.

observed, and be consistently applied. The problems of using even simple standard languages are compounded in comparative context. To repeat an earlier point, any measurement requires a common language with standard rules of interpretation. For example, let a person who has a formal right to participate in making authoritative decisions binding on some collectivity be a "politician" and let a person who can make decisions only over matters proscribed by rules and regulations be an "administrator." Because the idiom of particular political systems defines these positions differently, comparing the ratios of politicians to administrators is highly problematic. One alternative is to use standards specific to each country. These standards would be based on the constitutional provisions of India or Yugoslavia. But the use of these system-specific rules would make cross-national comparisons of such ratios impossible. A common language had not been applied. These specific languages of measurement could lead only to descriptive statements, such as "in the Yugoslav context there are so many administrators and so many politicians." This kind of statement, however, can be understood only if the context of Yugoslavia is understood.

The requirements of direct measurement satisfy a commonsense desire to get the "true" measure—the true number of politicians and administrators. But the concrete, specific nature of such measurement constitutes an obstacle to cross-national generality. In direct measurement one cannot make inferences from the concrete lists of administrators and politicians in the Yugoslav or Indian contexts to the underlying general context of the political roles of administrators and politicians. Definitions by fiat are arbitrarily true. But they are also less general.

The second requirement of direct measurement is that the language must express the relationships between classes of phenomena. Suppes and Zinnes state that the procedure of measurement must "characterize the formal properties of the empirical operations and relations used in the procedure and show that they are isomorphic to the appropriately chosen numerical operartions and relations." [10] Let us return to the example of politicians and administrators. Once the definition of these concepts has been stated in terms common to all systems, the grammar of the language must be chosen. In one country it may not be possible for an individual to be both a politician and an administrator because of legal or customary prohibitions. In another country there may be no such restrictions. The simplest grammar in the first case would be disjunctive: *if A, then not B, and, if B, then not A.* In the second case the necessary grammar would be alternative: *A and not B, and B and not A, and A and B.* In fact it would not be legitimate to use the first grammar for both countries, whereas

---

[10] Suppes and Zinnes, *op. cit.*, p. 4.

the second grammar would be appropriate for both. In terms of this general grammar, it is a matter of indifference that one country has a prohibition against dual positions and the other does not. Use of the alternative grammar does not distort the characteristics of the observations in the system in which an individual cannot occupy both positions. If the prohibition were abolished in the first country and established in the second, this grammar would still be appropriate. The nature of the data and the rules of interpretation contained in the language interact in necessitating a particular grammar.

According to the third requirement, the rules of empirical interpretation of the terms of a language must be applied consistently to all observations. In our example, these rules flow from the definitions of politicians and administrators. To the extent that the rules are not applied consistently, there is a loss in reliability. To the extent that inconsistent application of the rules tends to be concentrated in one country rather than be distributed across all countries, there is a *systematic* error in observations. Such error must be removed if the findings are to be reliable.

It is possible to use different rules of interpretation and to translate between them. For example, if positions $A, B, \ldots, N$ were coded "politician" for one set of observations and positions $A, B, \ldots, N, O, P$ for another set, it would be simple to make these two sets of rules interchangeable by either adding O and P to the first set or subtracting the same from the second set. Unless this is done, the two sets of observations cannot be used for comparative analysis.

Most of the preceding discussion was based on the nominal scale of measurement.[11] Direct measurement, however, can be formulated in terms of other types of scales. In ordinal scales, objects are ranked on some underlying dimension of magnitude. If all objects are ranked together regardless of the social system to which they belong, measurement is expressed in a standard language, a language external to any particular system. Within this language comparisons are legitimate. A typical application of ordinal scales is exemplified by studies of exposure to mass media in general or political news in particular.[12] Respondents in different countries are asked how frequently they follow political news: "never," "once a month," "at least weekly," or "everyday." The frequencies of the respondents who locate themselves in these ordered categories are then reported for each system and compared. These comparisons are legitimate,

[11] For a discussion of various kinds of scales, see W. S. Torgerson, *Theory and Methods of Scaling*, John Wiley & Sons, New York, 1968.

[12] See, for example, G. A. Almond and Sidney Verba, *The Civic Culture*, Princeton University Press, Princeton, N.J., 1963.

however, only if the ordering is made in terms of magnitudes having a physical rather than merely a psychological interpretation. Thus if frequency of exposure is measured in terms of physical time—days, weeks, and months—the language can be assumed to be standard. If, however, the categories use psychological time—"seldom," "from time to time," "often"—it is likely that the ordering is not invariant with regard to the culture. The judgment involved here requires a self-comparison of the respondent with the other members of the group or with the group norms. A university professor may perceive weekly reading of a newspaper to be "seldom," while a peasant may think it is "often." The invariance of the order of categories used in ordinal measurement is rarely a subject of explicit discussion in cross-national research, and hence many cross-national comparisons appear to be doubtful.[13]

In interval scales the problem is to assign numbers to various points on a measuring instrument. The system of numbers expresses equal intervals of the underlying magnitude. One of the most extensive uses of this kind of scale in cross-national research is Cantril's "self-anchoring scale," designed to measure magnitudes of hopes and aspirations for self and country. This scale was designed to allow each individual, regardless of culture or country, to define for himself where he stands now, where he was in the past, and where he believes he will be in the future. Eleven categories are displayed as a "ladder" and numbered from "0" to "10." The respondent is asked: "Here is a picture of a ladder. Suppose we say that the top of the ladder *(pointing)* represents the best possible life for you and the bottom *(pointing)* represents the worst possible life for you. Where on the ladder *(moving finger rapidly up and down ladder)* do you feel you personally stand at the present time?" The same question was used to obtain the individual's perception of where he stood five years ago and where he expected to be five years in the future.[14] Describing the instrument, Cantril stated:

"It should be emphasized over and over again that the ratings people assign either themselves or their nation are entirely subjective; hence a rating of say '6,' given by one person by no means indicates the same thing as a '6' given by another person. This obvious point is mentioned here because experience has shown that some people misunderstand the whole rationale of this technique assuming that the scale is like an intelligence test

[13] For an example of an instrument based on ordering that is cross-nationally invariant, see C. E. Ramsey and Jenaro Collazo, "Some Problems of Cross-Cultural Measurement," *Rural Sociology, 25, 1960.

[14] Hadley Cantril, *Patterns of Human Concern,* Rutgers University Press, New Brunswick, N.J., 1965, p. 23.

where a given rating has a precise and presumably somewhat universal connotation."[15]

The self-anchoring scale is a magnitude model. Each of the 11 points on the ladder is assigned a number that represents a unique, known, and constant amount of the quantity of hopes and aspirations. In spite of the warning, the self-anchoring scale is treated as if it had interval properties. A response of "6" in India, the United States, and Israel is treated as a "6" in a standard language. Otherwise means of countries could not have been compared. The observations expressed in the language of the ladder constitute direct measurement in which the language is consistently applied across cultures. Although consistently applied across cultures, the language of measurement is not standard. For it is clear that a "6" may express one quantity in one country and a different quantity in another.

In general the variety of social contexts within which measurement is conducted imposes serious limitations on direct measurement procedures. Direct measurement is immediately dependent upon specific observations and hence is highly sensitive to the differences of social contexts.

Inferred Measurement: System Validity and System Interference

Inferred measurement statements are based on social and behavioral laws. In assessing psychological dispositions, responses to questions are used to infer magnitudes of attitudes. Slips of the tongue are used to infer anxiety. In the assessment of characteristics of collectivities, riots may be used to infer political instability, and casual comments in official newspapers become the basis for inferring a policy change. In this kind of measurement concepts are again defined by fiat, but direct observations are combined with general laws to infer the presence or the magnitude of properties. The definition of the concept is not coterminous with any set of direct observations. On the contrary direct observations enter measurement statements only indirectly through inference based on general propositions.[16] In this context direct observations indicate meaning; they do not proscribe the limits of meaning.

Inferred measurement has the following components:
Definition: Let S be defined as X.
Proposition: All objects and only those objects that have property X are likely (certain) to have properties $x_1, x_2, \ldots, x_k$.

---

[15] *Ibid.*, p. 23.

[16] This is the kind of measurement referred to by "constructs." Although a construct is defined, it is assessed only through indicators. For a brief statement on the procedures used to determine the validity of constructs, see W. A. Scott and Michael Wertheimer, *Introduction to Psychological Research*, John Wiley & Sons, New York, 1962, Chap. 6.

Direct measurement procedures: $x_1, x_2, \ldots, x_k$ can be observed in the following ways. . . .

Composition rule: $x_1, x_2, \ldots, x_k$ interact in such a way that they can be combined by the following rule or rules. . . .

Rule of inference to property: Any object that was observed to have a certain amount of $x_1, x_2, \ldots, x_k$ is likely (certain) to have a specific amount of property X.

The result of combining direct observations $x_1, x_2, \ldots, x_k$ is the basis for inferring the magnitude of property X.[17] A rule of inference frequently used is a monotonic, linear one that states that any increase in the score indicates a corresponding, one-to-one, increase in the property. This rule of correspondence, of course, is only one of many. The relationship could be monotonic but not linear, that is, it could be a step or a curvilinear function. In practice some of the steps listed above are not made explicit. Nonetheless each of the components is present in any assessment by inference.

A measurement statement is thus a singular proposition that states that a specific object of observation has a given amount of a certain property. For example, statements that "Panama has an unstable political system" and "Respondent 173 has an authoritarianism score of 55 interval units" are measurement statements. They are inferred from the statements reporting the results of direct observations $x_1, x_2, \ldots, x_k$ on the basis of the general proposition and the inference rule. A specific measurement statement is thus obtained in the following way:

Direct measurement statement: An object A obtained the score of a as the result of the combination of direct measurements $x_1, x_2, \ldots, x_k$.

General proposition including an inferential rule: All objects and only those objects that have an amount a^* of property X will obtain a score of a as the combined result of operations $x_1, x_2, \ldots, x_k$.

Inferred measurement statement: Therefore, the object A has the amount a^* of property X.

The conclusion of this inference is the measurement statement. The relationship between the score a and the amount a^* of property X is ruled by the inferential rules discussed above.

Propositions used for inferences should be viewed in probabilistic rather

---

[17] For a discussion of composition rules, see May Brodbeck, "Methodological Individualisms: Definition and Reduction," *Philosophy of Science,* **25,** 1958.

than in deterministic terms.[18] In probabilistic terms each observation treated as an indicator would contain a "true" and an "error" component. If observations are accurate, the error is a function of the probable truth value of the social law on the basis of which the inference is made. If agreement with a question is assumed to indicate an attitude but it also reflects acquiescence, then measurement statements will contain error. Although inferred measurement recognizes inferential error, the language of direct measurement does not express this type of error. A response to a question is treated as a precise measure, but what that response indicates can be stated in probabilities.

A probabilistic measurement language can be based on several laws or hypotheses—on several indicators. The hypothesis that is to be tested is that a score on a particular indicator does indeed contribute to a composite score that corresponds to a magnitude of a property. If both the property as well as several indicators of it could be observed, then it would be possible to validate externally the indicators. Social scientists, however, confront quite a different situation. It is rarely possible to observe general concepts of presumed theoretical importance, such as aspirations, stability, or status. These can be "seen" only through indicators. This fact poses special difficulties in comparative research.

The basic problem of inferred measurement is the validity of the inferences from the reports of direct observations to measurement statements. When clear external criteria are not available, the researcher must appraise the validity of the indicators indirectly. Initially at least, this appraisal is of a judgmental or "face validity" nature. Judgments concerning face validity are the basis for treating the number of hospital beds as an indicator of government effectiveness. The choice of particular indicators is not completely arbitrary since it reflects the state of development of theory in a given area of social science. Had a general conceptual map been accepted in the social sciences, the rules for selection of indicators would have been available. To the extent that various groups of scientists operate with distinct conceptual frameworks and distinct theories linking concepts and the indicators, however, face validity remains a matter of personal or group judgment. The question whether voting turnout is a valid indicator of egalitarian pressures is largely unresolvable. One could at the most argue that this observable phenomenon has been used several times to indicate a different concept—political participation—and therefore it cannot be used as an indicator of egalitarian pressures within the same theory. The empirical

[18] These are probabilistic models. See W. A. Scott, "Attitude Measurement," in Gardner Lindzey and Elliot Aronson, eds., *Handbook of Social Psychology*, Vol. 2, Addison-Wesley, Reading, Mass., 1968.

criterion of "discriminant validity" is used here to isolate such observable phenomena that indicate one and only one general concept.[19]

In addition to face validity, another common criterion involves the "internal validity" of the indicators themselves. Here reliability of the indicators is used to infer their validity. The logic of this procedure is that if $x_1, x_2 \ldots, x_k$ are all indicators of X, that is, if each indicator is related to the presence or the magnitude of X, then $x_1, x_2 \ldots, x_k$ should be interrelated. In other words if x_1 is positively related to X and x_2 is positively related to X, their mutual dependence on X should be reflected in their interdependence. If both hospital beds and collection of taxes are related to governmental effectiveness, then effective governments should have *both* a large number of hospital beds and a large amount of collected taxes. If this assumption is false—the indicators are not mutually intercorrelated—it is clear that as a set they indicate more than one general concept. Therefore inferences based on the proposition that all indicators are a function of a single property X are invalid. If the assumption is correct, one test of validity of any single indicator becomes how it is correlated with all other indicators.

Procedurally, a set of indicators is established by (1) postulating a set of relationships of specific indicators with the general property being measured, (2) collecting data for the units under study, (3) intercorrelating the indicators (any number of expressions of relationships can be used), (4) excluding indicators that do not correlate highly with the other indicators, and (5) combining the values of the indicators selected by summating, weighting, and so forth, for a composite measure of the general property. Examples of this procedure are given in the following chapter.

In a comparative or cross-systemic context, validity means that we are measuring in *each system* under consideration what we intended to measure. The instrument designed for measurement of political participation must refer to those phenomena that constitute political participation in the Soviet Union and in the United States. But political participation of a Soviet and of an American citizen obviously is not expressed in terms of the same behavior. A politically active Russian would be concerned about the success of economic plans and would attend courses to develop his ideological consciousness. An American may do such things as wear a button in his lapel or donate money to a political party. Social systems influence the

---

[19] The underlying idea of discriminant validity is that indicators of the same property measured in different ways should be interrelated higher than indicators of different phenomena measured in the same way. See D. T. Campbell and D. W. Fiske, "Convergent and Discriminant Validation by the Multitrait-multimethod Matrix," *Psychological Bulletin*, **56**, 1959.

behavior of indicators, and therefore inferences made from indicators to concepts must be modified according to the system in which they were observed.

If the concept is "volume of transactions," the flow of money between individuals and institutions may be an adequate indicator in one social system but in another it may be imperative to count the number of non-monetary exchanges. If the concept is "community activeness," building highways may be a valid indicator in one system while inoculating cattle may be such in another. If the concept is attitude of "egalitarianism," feelings toward Negroes may be a valid indicator in one culture but its counterpart in another would be feelings toward underprivileged castes. These are examples of what we will call "system interference," a factor to be contended with in almost all comparative research.

System interference occurs when the inferences from the same direct measurement statements to inferred measurement statements are not equally valid in all systems under investigation. For example, a declaration by a respondent that he would object to his son marrying an offspring of a supporter of a certain political party is not an equally valid basis in all countries for inferring "political partisanship" defined as the "psychological distance between or among parties."[20] In the United States, such an inference may be valid, while in Italy the underlying attitude may be the authoritarianism of family rather than perceived distance between parties. In other words, in the United States the answer "yes, I would object" may indicate with a high probability the perceived distance between parties, whereas in Italy an objection to such a marriage would not reflect perceived distance between parties.

A system is a set of elements that are interdependent: a change in any one element has some probability of changing any other element. Although the patterns of interaction among the elements of a system may be described in general terms, the behavior of any specific component or "trait" is determined by other components. When these specific components or traits are used as indicators of some general phenomena, they are taken out of the context of the system to which they belong. For example, it is obvious that the systemic context determines whether voting is a valid indicator of participation. In one political system voting may be a choice between alternatives and in another an expression of solidarity. The interdependence

[20] The psychological distance between parties and this measure of it is presented in G. A. Almond and Sidney Verba, *op. cit.*

within a system is the core of the functionalist position, which argues that social systems or cultures can be compared only as total units because removing any particular trait out of context is both misleading and invalid.[21]

It is necessary in comparative measurement to vary the propositions used for inferences so that the validity of measurement statements is maintained in each system. This can be done only by reference to the systemic context of observations used in an inferred measurement statement. When inferences are made from the volume of a substance to the temperature of the air surrounding it, rules of inference must be relative to the pressure of the atmosphere. Although these adjustments may be an infrequent and uncomplicated problem for the natural sciences, social scientists ordinarily make their observations within the context of a social system and the problem of systemic interference can almost never be avoided. Even context-free laboratory observations in the behavioral sciences are not as free as once thought, and it is not a matter of indifference where the laboratory observations are made.

The consequences of system interference are most striking when a phenomenon that is commonly present in one system cannot even be found in another system. Americans do not attend courses in ideological consciousness, do not dig manure pits, and do not sacrifice animals in religious ceremonies. Although these are examples of data produced by the social system independently of the efforts of scientists, the problem of the lack of comparable phenomena does not disappear when a researcher generates his own data. Certain questions, such as whether Peruvian peasants prefer compact or full-sized cars, cannot be asked in a particular social system because they are devoid of meaning and thus worthless as a basis of inference. In a less obvious sense, researchers often create phenomena that do not "exist." Indicators appear as an artifact of the observational procedures, such as asking a question whether an individual "checks more than twice if he is overstepping his tasks" in a culture that does not define individual tasks. A researcher can almost always obtain variance within a system when he generates his own data, even if it is only variance of error.

The proof that inferences in a measurement language are indeed free of systemic interference rests on the investigator. He ought to be sensitive to systemic interference even in seemingly homogeneous populations. As

---

[21] Although the emphasis on the interrelation of social phenomena goes back to early functionalists, this does not mean that the use of the concept of "system" necessitates accepting "functional explanation." We are using the concept of "system" as *any* distinct set of interrelated elements, not only as a set that contains mechanisms of self-regulation.

Allardt has observed, unemployment in Finland may indicate insecurity in rural settings but not in the cities. Finland is not a single system when unemployment is used as an indicator of insecurity.[22]

Equivalent Measurement Across Systems

The question of equivalence arises if and only if system interference is present and measurement involves inference. If "chief executive" is defined as a person who is either president, prime minister, or king, the only question is whether one of these three positions exists in a given system. If voting is defined as casting one's ballot in any formal election provided by law, the question of whether casting a ballot in that election is an "equivalent" measure of voting is meaningless. If any phenomenon is defined in terms of listing its observable manifestations (direct measurement), the question whether a definition is equivalent across different systems cannot even be formulated.

If system interference is present and measurement is based on inference, inferences valid in one system will not be equally valid in another system. The problem of measurement imposed by the combination of inference with system interference is that the *validity of measurement inferences is specific to each social system.* Inferences leading to measurement statements must be validated in each social system. Interaction of each property of the components of systems' with other properties must be taken into account. In other words, the inferences in the measurement language must consider the meaning or the context of a measured trait in terms of the pattern of systemic interactions of each system. Whereas in theory formulation the emphasis is placed on generality rather than accuracy, in measurement it is accuracy, not generality. Thus system-specific propositions that provide greater accuracy should be the dominant focus of measurement, as was argued in Part One.

Let us return to the example concerning psychological distance between parties. The observable behavior is the same: individuals in different systems answer the same question asked under the same conditions. As a result of these observations, each individual is given a score of political partisanship—the extent to which he perceives distance between or among parties.

---

[22] Eric Allardt, "Implications of Within Nation Variations and Regional Imbalances for Cross-National Research," in R. L. Merritt and Stein Rokkan, eds., *Comparing Nations: The Use of Quantitative Data in Cross-National Research,* Yale University Press, New Haven, Conn., 1966, pp. 337–58.

Country A	Country B
A person A answered "Yes."	A person B answered "Yes."

All persons and only those persons who perceive high distance between parties are likely (certain) to answer "Yes."
Therefore, it is highly likely (certain) that

Person A is "partisan"	Person B is "partisan"

The truth of the last statements, the inferred measurement statements, depends upon the truth of the general proposition that states that persons who say they would object to their son or daughter marrying a supporter of a different party are likely to be "partisans" regardless of the system to which they belong. But if system interference is present, then the general proposition is not equally true in both societies. The validity of the inference is not invariant across social systems.

If the same inferences are not equally valid for different societies, can measurement statements be compared across systems? If the same inferences lead to different results in different social systems, how can inference rules and measuring instruments be adjusted to produce equally valid results in differing social systems? This problem is so pervasive that it has led some social scientists to deny the nomothetic nature of the social sciences. But the validity of inferences can be made relative to each social system. For this purpose instruments based on different observations and inferences must obviously be used. If, however, different instruments are designed for particular systems, how can we know that what we are measuring is the same in all systems and thus comparable? In addition to being valid, instruments must be reliable across systems. In other words, the measuring instrument must yield consistent results regardless of the social system in which it has been applied.

Reliability is easier to assess than validity, and there are many methods for estimating it. Most of the estimations are based on the same fundamental assumption: measurement is reliable to the extent that the variance of the "true" scores approximates the observed variance.[23] If true variance is defined as the common variance, numerical expressions of reliability are avaialable. Although distributions of observations, the actual number of observations, and errors compound the problem of estimating reliability, we only want to know whether the results provided by an instrument can be reproduced by that instrument.

Measurement that satisfies the two conditions discussed above—validity in terms of each social system and reliability across social systems—will be called "equivalent measurement." It should be emphasized that this concept of equivalence does not refer to observations but only to the results of inferences made from those observations, that is, the inferred measurement statements. An instrument is equivalent across systems to the extent that the *results* provided by the instrument reliably describe with (nearly) the same validity a particular phenomenon in different social systems. In a questionnaire it is not relevant whether the stimuli were the same or whether a question was well translated from one language to another. What is important is whether this question as asked allows for a valid inference to the same underlying properties regardless of the social system. *Stimulus equivalence is an important problem only if measurement does not involve inference.*[24] In inferred measurement, stimulus equivalence is of secondary importance. The focus must be placed on the equivalence of inferences made from observations.

Some auxiliary notions are needed in order to understand this concept of equivalence. If we wanted to measure the verbal facility of all people in all countries of the world, every language in the world could conceivably enter our measure. The domain of the concept, what the concept refers to, is the facility to use all words in all languages in the world. All words in all languages would be the total population of indicators. But it is quite clear that measuring the verbal facility of Americans in Hindi would not be appropriate. For each language there is a corresponding population of individuals. Any specific language can be viewed as a set of indicators that can be utilized to measure the verbal facility of a set of individuals. In order to construct a measurement instrument of verbal facility in each language, a sample of the words from that language, a subpopulation of indicators, may be taken. If we are measuring the verbal facility of Americans, we may take several samples of 100 English words and test how many of them each individual knows.

In general terms, we are measuring a property denoted by a concept. First we defined the domain of the concept or, in other words, we specified the population of indicators for all systems. These indicators, however, may not be equally relevant or even present in every social system. If they are not, it is necessary to identify the *subpopulation of indicators relative to each social system.* We can then draw samples of indicators from these subpopulations to be used as specific instruments in each system.

In practice this definition of equivalence does not require that the total population of indicators be located. In the example above the procedure

[24] Thus, in our view, the customary emphasis on equivalence of stimuli is misplaced. Interviewer training, time, and manner in which the interviews are conducted and even the formulation of questions need not be identical. Stimulus equivalence should be viewed solely from the point of view of equivalence of the resulting measurement statements.

was first to describe the total population of indicators, all words in all languages in use, and then to examine what subpopulations of this universe, specific languages, could be found for sets of individuals belonging to specific systems. If it were necessary to know the total population of indicators, then substantial research would be required before any property could be assessed. It is possible to start with specific social systems and to generate a sample of indicators for each of them: "In India authoritarianism is indicated by... ; in the United States authoritarianism is indicated by. . . ." When this process is completed, it would be possible to identify which indicators of the total set are invariant across social systems and which are relative to particular systems. Even in our example of constructing an instrument for verbal facility across systems, it may be found that, as a result of diffusion, certain words would be common for several languages.

This procedure for constructing equivalent measures across systems enables the context of a system to enter the process of measurement. System-specific statements, such as "in Egypt bowing is an expression of deference," become part of the measuring instrument. The indicators hypothesized for each system are assumed to be a sample of indicators for each system, and each of these system-specific samples is assumed to be a sample of the total population of indicators. If some indicators are considered relevant in *all* systems under study, they can be treated, at least initially, as "system-free" indicators. If the samples of indicators have an overlapping or system-free subset, the procedure for establishing equivalence can combine system-free and system-specific indicators into an equivalent and thus comparable measure. This procedure will be discussed in the following chapter.

A different situation arises when samples of indicators derived from particular systems do not overlap. Is it still possible to treat the scores based on two independent samples of indicators as equivalent? First, if the scores were based on a true random sample of the total population of indicators, it would be possible to translate the score from one sample of indicators to a score based on another sample. If 1000 questions constituted the total population of indicators of numerical ability and a group of students were tested on a random sample of a 100 problems, their scores would be the same regardless of which sample of 100 questions was used. The samples of indicators would be interchangeable. If a student received a score of X on a randomly drawn test of 100 questions, he should receive the same score on any other test of 100 randomly drawn questions. Each test can then be interchanged with any other test.

The hard test of the equivalence of instruments is the interchangeability of their results. *Instruments are equivalent if and only if some rules are available by which the measurement statements produced by them can be interchanged without changing their logical value.* In other words, instruments are equivalent if the truth or falsity of statements derived from these instruments is invariant with respect to their structure. If a score resulting from the application of one instrument predicts the score resulting from the application of another instrument, then the instruments are equivalent. Since measurement involves error, we should use a probabilistic language: the scores on one test need only predict with some probability rather than determine the scores on another test.

Within the same culture this concept of equivalence is intuitively clear, and direct tests can be applied to check whether any pair of instruments is indeed equivalent. But can the instruments used to test verbal facility in Swedish and English ever be interchanged? Is it at least *logically* possible that they can be interchanged? The answer to the first question is clearly negative. If an American does not speak Swedish, his verbal facility score in Swedish will yield a trivial prediction of his verbal facility, a score of zero. The answer to the second question is positive. It is logically possible that these two instruments could be interchanged in such a way that a person with a given verbal facility would score in the same way regardless of the language of the test. This statement is based on the postulate of substitutability presented in the first chapter: if the articulate Mr. Peterson were an equally verbal American, his scores on verbal facility in Swedish and English could be interchanged. The two instruments would therefore be equivalent. A procedure for establishing equivalence when no indicators are common will be elaborated in the next chapter.

Summary and Conclusions

The goal of science is to reduce the overwhelming number of specific observations into general statements. The first step toward this goal consists of ordering specific observations into a measurement system. Specific observations are made within the contexts of particular social systems. But if social science theories are to be general, it is necessary to move from these specific observations, relative to particular contexts, to general concepts invariant across systems. Therefore in most situations cross-system measurement should be based on inference from specific observations to general concepts. Such inference need not, however, be based on the same general propositions and, hence, need not involve common indicators. Measurement statements resulting from inference must preserve their truth-falsity value regardless of the instrument and the social system involved. The instruments that satisfy this condition are called equivalent. These instruments provide results valid in each system and stable across systems.

What is important about equivalence in cross-system research, however, is the invariance of the logical value of the measurement statements understood in probabilistic terms, not the exact comparability of the obtained scores. The sufficient criterion of equivalence is that in all systems the indicators allow us to infer with equal validity the magnitude of the general property. The criterion of strict interchangeability of the particular scores may turn out to be excessively stringent and unnecessary in most situations of cross-system measurement.

The scores can be interchanged if and only if a transformation rule is available that enables a score on one instrument to be expressed in terms of the scale of another instrument. In order to identify such a transformation rule, the properties of each scale must be known. For example, to transform the scores from one interval scale developed for Brazilians to another one developed for Mexicans, two such properties of the scales must be known: (1) the size of the intervals and (2) their origin. Since this condition is highly restrictive, it is usually circumvented in comparative research by assuming that the intervals are the same in all systems and the origin of scales, if unknown, is common to all systems.[25]

It is important to recall that comparative analysis of *relationships within systems* does not require a knowledge of common origin or size of intervals. This is necessary only for descriptive comparisons. Thus comparative analysis of relationships within systems demands *less powerful measurement instruments* than those disarming pieces of descriptive information that compare within-system parameters. Both the theoretical prospects and the costs of measurement should direct comparative research to comparisons of relationships within systems rather than of aggregated properties of systems.

Comparative research requires a strategy for establishing equivalence. The models of measurement based on inference provide a means to remove the multiplier effect of hundreds of social systems and thereby measure properties in terms free of the context of particular systems. The strategy proposed here in effect holds the social system constant by adapting the bases for inference so that the impact of the social system can be removed. It provides a basis for validly coding the characteristics of specific systems into a common idiom, a language of generality. This was the insight and impact of the early functionalists—to reduce social diversity into a general language. To that end they talked about functional equivalence, but did so without the benefit of an explicit language of measurement. But equivalence requires systematic criteria derived from a language of science. With systematic criteria, measurement can be freed from the bias of specific investi-

[25] This is assumed, for example, in R. D. Meade and J. O. Whittaker, "A Cross-Cultural Study of Authoritarianism," *Journal of Social Psychology*, **72**, 1967.

gators and verification by authority and can enter the public domain of scientific inquiry.

CHAPTER SIX

Establishing Equivalence

A General Criterion of Equivalence. The Place of Multiple Indicators.
Indicator Distribution: Conditions of Establishing Equivalence.
Common Indicators Only. Common and System-Specific Indicators.
System-Specific Indicators Only. Summary and Conclusions.

To establish the equivalence of measurement instruments, they must be tested according to some criteria. Such criteria can be met by following certain procedures. The procedures that should be followed to determine equivalence depend on the nature of the available indicators. Three types of procedures designed to test equivalence will be presented below.

The question of equivalence is meaningful only when inferences are made from specific observations to general properties. In comparative research, this problem arises because it is unlikely that the same bases of inference are equally valid for all systems. The importance of developing criteria for establishing equivalence was underlined by Sears several years ago:

"The criteria for determining conceptual equivalence of responses are not at all clear. However, the problem is probably no worse at the cross-cultural level than at the inter-individual. For example, one might ask what criteria there are for defining both a street fight and the telling of malicious gossip as indices of aggression. We seem to accept this identity on some intuitive basis and without critical examination of the criteria involved. Equally, we have to this point accepted reasonably obvious similarities cross-culturally, doubtless on the same intuitive basis. Actually, of course, intuition is merely a word to indicate that our reasoning and observations on this matter have been unsystematic. If we are to go beyond the few concepts which many students of behavior have been examining and working with for many years, however, these criteria must be formalized."[1]

We have defined the equivalence of measurement instruments in terms of invariance of measurement statements. If one instrument produces the same results as another, the two are equivalent. Therefore, in order to determine whether instruments are equivalent, it is necessary to have a set of rules by which the results from one instrument can be transformed into the results of the other.

In practice, however, the interchangeability of the results from two instruments can rarely be directly tested. In our example of verbal facility it is possible only to *infer* that the scores in the Swedish and English tests are interchangeable. There is no way of administering a test of verbal facility in English to a Swede. The problem then is to find some criteria that can be used as a basis for *inferring* whether or not two or more instruments meet these criteria, that is, whether it is highly probable that the results produced by them are indeed interchangeable. Unless some valid cross-system empirical criterion is found (predictor validity), the criteria for inferring the equivalence of measurement instruments will have to be found in the instruments themselves. This means that we have to look at the indicators that comprise the measuring instruments.

A General Criterion of Equivalence

The criterion for inferring the equivalence of measurement instruments can be found in the structure of the indicators. Equivalence of measurement instruments must be demonstrated when there is some reason for believing that system interference is present, that is, when the same inference cannot be used in all systems. What we are seeking in comparative research is a measure that is reliable across systems and valid within systems. The validity of indicators can be assessed indirectly from the homogeneity or reliability of the indicators within systems. Validity is system specific. The reliability of measurement instruments across systems can be inferred either from an analysis of the pooled population of all units of observation or, under some additional assumptions, from the relative reliability of indicators within particular systems.

In particular, whenever a number of indicators is common to all systems, a direct test of reliability across systems is available. This test consists of the observation of the correlations among indicators for the pooled popula-

[1] Robert Sears, "Transcultural Variables and Conceptual Equivalence," in Bert Kaplan, ed., *Studying Personality Cross-Culturally*, Row, Peterson, Evanston, Ill., 1961, p. 453.

tion of the units of observation. If these correlations are sufficiently high, that is, if the set of common indicators is reliable in the total, pooled population, cross-system reliability of this set is demonstrated. Validity within each system is inferred indirectly, on the basis of the assumptions discussed in the preceding chapter, from the intercorrelations of these indicators within each system. If these intercorrelations are similar and sufficiently high, the sets of indicators are considered equally valid for each system. If both common and system-specific indicators are available, the set of common indicators provides an anchor for ascertaining that the system-specific items correlated with the identical (reliable and common) indicators measure the same general property in all systems. If no common indicators are available, then cross-system reliability can be inferred only indirectly on the basis of theoretical assumptions concerning particular indicators and on the basis of similarity of the structure of correlations within each system.

It should be strongly emphasized that this procedure for testing equivalence is meaningful only in the context of explicit theoretical assumptions concerning the dimensions of the general property being examined and the behavior of specific indicators. The procedure consists of testing hypotheses that state, on the bases of some assumptions, that *if* the behavior of sets of indicators is the same in all systems, *then* these indicators permit inferences of equivalent measurement statements. The assumptions from which these hypotheses are derived combine general theoretical statements with singular premises concerning particular systems. Thus if we were concerned with deviant behavior in a system in which the norms prohibit premarital sex and adultery but would permit divorce and the remarriage of widows and in another system in which the norms would prohibit divorce and remarriage but permit premarital and extramarital sex, then measurement of normative integration of local communities within those systems would require the following steps:

(Assumptions)   Human beings ordinarily behave in accordance with the norms of their society, and in society A the norms prohibit premarital and extramarital sex, whereas in society B the norms prohibit divorce and remarriage;

therefore,   (Hypothesis)   If the incidence of premarital and the incidence of extramarital sexual relations are interrelated in society A and those of divorce and remarriage of widows are interrelated in society B, then these indicators of deviant behavior are equivalent,

and   (Test)   these indicators are similarly interrelated within those systems.

Therefore   (Inference)   these indicators are equivalent.

Although the concepts of reliability and validity are retained, this criterion of equivalence places emphasis on the validity within each system. The rationale for this focus is that measurement statements must be accurate and that the very idea of a system implies that relationships between indicators or variables within systems are to some extent relative to each system. When the validity of the inference cannot be conclusively determined, the only basis for determining equivalence is the behavior of the indicators within systems.

This view of equivalence, of course, assumes that the basic datum in comparative research is the within-system relationship. In order to establish the equivalence of measurement instruments it is necessary to have observations of some within-system units, such as individuals, groups, organizations, or local governments. The measurement statements will consequently be valid only for those units within particular systems.

This criterion of equivalence rests on two additional assumptions. The first is that, for each system being analyzed, there is some chance that the units can vary on the general property being measured. For most properties the possibility of within-system variation is relatively obvious, and in some cases the absence of any chance for any set of objects to vary is equally clear. For example, in some systems there is no norm (law) allowing for local autonomy in collecting revenues. It would be inappropriate to try to establish valid indicators of such local autonomy. In this case there is a general characteristic of the system, absence of local autonomy in revenue collection, and zero variance within this system. We cannot, in short, observe indicators of local autonomy within this system. Less obvious is the case of properties for which the researcher generates the data. He may be looking for valid items to assess the perceptions of villagers of the benefits received from the national government when there is either no perception of a national government or no admissible perception of a benign national government. Yet error contained in the observations may result in individual variation on these perceptions.

The second assumption is that the indicators found in any system constitute a sample of the universe of all indicators of a particular property. For any property there is a domain of indicators. The domain contains the universe of indicators. Any specific measurement instrument is made of a sample of this universe of indicators. Thus this assumption states that the indicators found in a particular system constitute a "true" sample of the total number of indicators of the property in all systems. The tenability of this assumption for any particular set of indicators can be evaluated in terms of the number of indicators identified in each system. The greater the number of indicators that can be hypothesized to measure a general property in each of the systems under study, the greater the probability that the indicators for each system approximate a sample of the universe of indicators. The importance of this assumption for establishing the equivalence of measurement instruments is derived from another assumption: to the extent that the indicators of a general property in each system approach a sample of the universe of indicators, the structure of the indicators across systems will be similar.

The similarity of the structure of indicators is the criterion for establishing the equivalence of measurement instruments. The similarity of structure can be defined in terms of the patterns of intercorrelations among indicators. If the indicators for particular systems, hypothesized to belong to the domain of the same concept, are intercorrelated with each other in the same way in each system, the structure of the indicators is said to be the same. The measurement statements based on these indicators can be inferred to be equivalent. Technically a decision that the structures of indicators are the same for instruments used in different systems may be based either on comparisons of correlation matrices for each system or other forms of patterns of interrelationships, such as factorial structures.

The Place of Multiple Indicators

Because the criterion of equivalence has been defined as the similarity of the structure of indicators, it is necessary to have a set of indicators for each system. The behavior of these *sets* of indicators is the basis for evaluating the equivalence of the measurement statements.

The extent to which a set of indicators for any system approximates a random sample of the universe of indicators of a property implies the extent of similarity in their structures. In one sense the test of the equivalence of two measuring instruments is whether the indicators selected for each system are a random sample of the universe of indicators for all systems. Rather than compare characteristics of the sample with characteristics of the universe, however, what is compared is the behavior of two or more samples.

Intuitive judgments about equivalent indicators must be subjected to examination. Generally there are two bases for discussing an intuitive judgment concerning the equivalence of measurement instruments. The first is that one or more items in two measurement instruments are presumed to be "identical" because the same indicators are used in all systems. The second is more intuitive, in the sense discussed by Sears. On the basis of knowledge of two systems, "malicious gossip" and a "street fight" are hypothesized to be equivalent indicators of aggression. In the latter case the equivalence of the measurement statements derived from the two indicators is often argumentatively established on the basis of some "understanding" of the systems involved. But the former case, in which the measuring statements are assumed to be equivalent because the indicators are identical, is equally problematical. If we had correctly observed a street fight in two countries, the inferences derived from direct measurement statements that a street fight is a sign of aggression in both systems would be treated with as much circumspection as the statement that in one culture a street fight is an indicator of "aggression" whereas in another culture "aggression" is indicated by malicious gossip. Whether the indicators are "identical" is not the problem. What is at issue are the measurement statements resulting from the use of the indicators. *Equivalence is a matter of inference, not of direct observations.*

The use of single indicators in measurement often obscures the problem of equivalence. Cantril, for example, uses the structure of a self-anchored scale, a ladder, to assess aspirations for self and country.[2] As we have seen, he makes the assumption of a common origin when he compares mean scores across countries. But he also assumes that properties of the ladder are system-free across all countries; that a response of "6" in one country is equivalent to a response of "6" in another; that the space between the steps of the ladder, five years, and the words "hope," "fear," and so forth, allow for the same inferences regardless of system. Even if it were true that a response of "6" in one country is a response of "6" in another, it would still not be clear whether the inferences that can be made are the same, interchangeable, and thus equivalent.

Indeed, in most cross-national or cross-cultural surveys stimulus identity, insofar as it can be established, is used as the basis for legitimizing the use of a common inference rule. Almond and Verba establish the validity of most of their measures in terms of what they consider to be "identical" measurement instruments.[3] Insofar as these measurement statements are interpreted only as responses expressed in a standard language of direct measurement, there really is no question of their comparability, only arguments about the similarity of the stimuli. When these direct measurement statements, however, are used to infer general properties, such as the previously discussed "psychological distance between parties," the validity of the inference must be established. The argument is with the inference rule being used: that common, direct measurement instruments permit automatically similar inferences. But in order to test the validity of this law of

[2] Hadley Cantril, *Patterns of Human Concern,* Rutgers University Press, New Brunswick, N.J., 1965.

[3] G. A. Almond and Sidney Verba, *The Civic Culture,* Princeton University Press, Princeton, N.J., 1963.

social science measurement, it is necessary to have several indicators of the same phenomena or other criteria of validation. And the need for establishing equivalence of measurement statements, as Sears points out, is probably no more problematic for a study of Russians and Americans than for one of American whites and blacks.

Researchers are generally concerned with developing equivalent measurement instruments, not with testing the equivalence of the instruments already used. Developing equivalent measurement instruments is a process of inquiry by which equivalence is assessed at various stages. In this context three general situations will be discussed, each opening up alternative strategies for devising different, but equivalent, instruments.

Indicator Distribution: Conditions of Establishing Equivalence

The situations faced by researchers in establishing the equivalence of measurement instruments depend upon the distribution of indicators across systems and upon languages in which indicators are expressed. In order to specify the nature of the problem, definitions of *common* and *identical* indicators will be introduced. An indicator is common when it is used in all systems and produces variance in all these systems. The number of murders in a local community will be a common indicator of normative integration if it is used in all systems. A particular set of responses to a question will be a common indicator if the question is applied to all respondents regardless of systems.

An identical indicator is a common indicator that indicates the same property across systems. This is a stringent condition because, as has been discussed in the previous chapter, saying "yes" to a question "means" different things in different cultures—the validity of an inference derived from an affirmative response varies across systems. Thus indicators that are common may not be identical. Commonality in terms of the language of direct measurement implies nothing about identity in terms of the language of inferred measurement.

There is, however, an intuitive presumption that an indicator that is applied in all systems is more likely to be equivalent than one that is not. Thus responses to a common question are more likely to be equivalent than responses to different questions. But even if this intuition is generally valid, it is still necessary to demonstrate that the same indicator leads to equivalent measurement statements.

The distribution of indicators determines the strategies that can be followed in developing equivalent measures across systems. This distribution is a function of the kinds of observations called for by the measuring instruments. The first type of situation occurs when common indicators are available. In this situation it is necessary to select from the samples of common indicators those that will result in equivalent measurement statements. The second situation occurs when the samples of indicators from each system overlap: some indicators are common, and some are specific to each system. The problem is to select those common indicators that are identical and to add system-specific indicators to develop equivalent measurement instruments. The third situation occurs when there is no overlap in the samples of indicators taken from each system. Each indicator is relative since it "belongs" to a particular system.

The distribution of the indicators depends not only upon the interaction between a theory and the nature of the social world but also on the methods by which observations are made. Typically, questionnaire data will express observations in a standard language, that is, they will contain a set of common indicators. If these indicators can be shown to produce equivalent measurement statements, they are identical. The task is to select and weigh common indicators so that they can be used to construct equivalent measurement instruments.

Some common and some specific indicators are often found in survey data when the specific context of questions has to be adapted to the systems under study. Thus, in measuring role satisfaction, it may be possible to use some common indicators, but it may also be necessary to vary the wording of certain questions in order to examine specific features of the role defined in terms of the system. This situation is also likely to occur if the indicators are produced and recorded by the social system—the indicators collected by various organizations for general use. Some of the indicators will be expressed in a standard language, such as gasoline consumption or the number of people per hectare; others will be specific to the system, such as the yield of sugar beets or the number of wells dug. In this case it is possible to combine common indicators with system-specific indicators.

The third type of situation is usually faced by social scientists studying characteristics of collectivities within systems. Often there is not a single common indicator. Each indicator is in some ways unique to the system. Furthermore, there is often no way in which observations expressed in one language can be transformed into a general or standard language, as can be done in transforming national income data into dollar units. This kind of situation is obvious when an observation possible in one system simply cannot be made in another. Local allocation of resources for police salaries simply does not take place in all countries. Even if the indicators appear to be common—for example, the number of robberies—there may be so much difference in the manner of observation that although the language is similar, the indicators cannot be considered as common.

Although there is a presumption that a common indicator has a better probability of being equivalent than two different indicators, the equivalence of measurement instruments of which the indicators are a part must still be demonstrated. The indicators, common or different, must be validated by their behavior within the system for which the instrument is designed. The context of the system is what is important. The presumption in favor of the equivalence of common indicators probably is not strong enough to justify any substantial effort to locate them.

What is perhaps of more importance than the presumption of equivalence of common indicators is that a set of *identical* indicators in two measurement instruments can provide an anchor for evaluating the behavior of each measurement instrument. But whether this added bit of information is worthwhile is a matter that must be justified in terms of a specific research problem.

Common Indicators Only

If a theory concerning a given realm of investigation and the availability of data permit using common indicators in all systems, it is sufficient to demonstrate that these indicators are identical. For if a set of common indicators is shown to be identical across systems, the criterion of equivalence has been met. The measurement statements resulting from these indicators are invariant across systems. In this case, system interference—the source of the problem of equivalence—is not present.

The hypothesis tested in this situation states that there is no system interference and hence, if the common indicators satisfy certain tests, they permit inferring equivalent statements. Two tests are necessary. First, it must be shown that the indicators behave in the same way in all systems. An ideal case in which the structures of interrelations among three indicators are identical in three systems is illustrated below:

Correlation Among Indicators

	System I				System II				System III		
	x_1	x_2	x_3		x_1	x_2	x_3		x_1	x_2	x_3
x_1	1.00	.40	.50	x_1	1.00	.40	.50	x_1	1.00	.40	.50
x_2		1.00	.50	x_2		1.00	.50	x_2		1.00	.50
x_3			1.00	x_3			1.00	x_3			1.00

If these correlations are identical, and the variances in each system are approximately the same, it is highly likely that the magnitude of the correlations within these systems will equal the magnitude of the correlations for the pooled population. However, as we have seen in Chapter Three, this may not always be true. Thus a second test is necessary, one that examines the correlations among the indicators in the pooled population. This test provides a direct assessment of cross-system reliability of the common indicators.

In this example, there is no system interference. But this kind of situation will rarely be found in research conducted in several systems. If a very large number of indicators is examined, it may be possible to find an adequately reliable set of indicators. But in attempting to obtain similar correlations within systems, many common indicators will have to be discarded, and those retained will not be the ones most highly correlated within each system.

An alternative is to adjust the indicators so that system interference is minimized. In order to determine which indicators are most affected by systemic factors, it is necessary to have some measure of the factors that are introducing system interference into the inferences. The goal need not be to eliminate system interference altogether, but rather to reduce it to tolerable proportions.

One type of measurement instruments in which system bias has been persistently controversial is intelligence tests. Differences found between blacks and whites and among social groups have been attributed to the general "cultural" bias in the instruments. Again, the issue is not whether members of one group score lower or higher than members of another, but the inferences made from this fact.

Cattell and his associates have attempted to remove the cultural bias from intelligence tests.[4] The problem was to define the nature of the cultural bias and to develop a "culture fair" intelligence test. Culture fair means that not all bias has been removed. Cattell reasons that if intelligence is defined as the ability to learn or solve problems rather than what has been learned, then two separate dimensions (factors) should be identifiable in the responses to intelligence tests: (1) the ability to learn, or intellectual facility, and (2) what has been learned. What has been learned is subject to cultural bias, the opportunities and social rewards for learning. Cattell designated the first type of responses as "fluid intelligence," the other as "crystallized intelligence." These two types of response patterns were

---

[4] R. B. Cattell, "Theory of Fluid and Crystallized Intelligence: A Critical Experiment," *Journal of Educational Psychology*, **54**, 1963. For a general discussion of this approach and reports on cross-cultural findings, see R. B. Cattell, "Are I.Q. Tests Intelligent?," *Psychology Today*, **1**, 1968.

isolated by examining the structure of responses to test items through factor analysis.

Even if the nature of cultural bias has been identified and isolated in response patterns, it is still necessary to demonstrate that the measurement statements resulting from indicators of fluid intelligence are equivalent across systems. A criterion of equivalence must be defined. Because Cattell is interested in characterizing populations rather than in explaining relationships between variables within systems, his criteria for determining that the instruments are free from system interference are identical means and variances for each culture. The similarity of means and standard deviations is the basis for inferring that the tests of fluid intelligence, based on common indicators, will produce equivalent measurement statements. As evidence that the test is culturally unbiased (culture fair), he presents data from a study by Rodd that show the near similarities in means and standard deviations for American and Chinese (Hong Kong) students. The critical issue in this procedure is the criterion of equivalence used by Cattell. It is based on an empirical assumption, not about the general behavior of indicators in measurement, but about the nature of intelligence around the world.

A second strategy for establishing the equivalence of measurement instruments based on multiple common indicators within systems is to adjust the scores of some systems so that they will be "like" the scores of the systems with which they are to be compared. In this way the impact of system interference on the measures can be reduced. There are no familiar examples of this in cross-national or cross-cultural research. As a hypothetical example, let us assume that we want to develop an instrument to measure the resource allocations of American states and that there is "North-South" interference. If there were several indicators of expenditure patterns available, we could partial out at least the major interfering factor. We could find the best predictor (discriminator) of the northern and southern states, say percentage of nonwhite population, and partial out the influence of this factor from the intercorrelations among the indicators. In cross-national applications, a variable could be selected that best predicts (discriminates) the regional configuration in each country, and intercorrelations among indicators could be examined when the influence of these "extraneous" factors, leading to system interferences, is reduced. In this way, we could reduce some "historical" system interferences in inference by adjusting scores within each system.

Although this strategy is not often followed, it could further comparative analysis between systems when the influence of some specific systemic factor were known. Generally what is done, however, is to examine the influence of these factors when testing theories across systems along the lines suggested in Part One. But the measurement option is also open. By following it we could identify a common set of indicators that are identical in all systems under study when systemic influences are removed.

Common and System-Specific Indicators

The second situation is encountered when there is a set of common indicators, but not enough of them behave identically to provide satisfactory reliability and validity. Reliability, it should be recalled, is a function both of the strength of relationships among indicators and the number of indicators. This situation is likely to arise either when an attempt is made to develop a scale on the basis of common indicators and the set of identical indicators turns out to be small or when, for theoretical reasons, the use of specific indicators seems necessary. It often seems advisable, particularly in attitude measurement, to use questions of different levels of abstractness, from general declarative statements to descriptions of specific hypothetical situations. Such a procedure permits a "correlational control of meaning." [5] For example, in attempting to ascertain whether an individual is a "socialist," we may ask him questions requiring general self-identification but at the same time test whether he would approve specific socialist norms under particular sets of circumstances. It is most likely, however, that the specific situations cannot be the same in different cultures, and hence the formulation of the questions will have to vary. In general if there is a set of common indicators that behave identically across systems but the number of items is too small to provide an acceptable level of reliability, system-specific indicators can be combined with the identical indicators to produce equivalent instruments.

This strategy was self-consciously followed in the International Studies of Values in Politics.[6] The goal was to obtain a measurement instrument that would assess the values of local political leaders in four countries. A pretest allowed the behavior of a common set of indicators to be observed across all countries and within each country. The value of "social harmony" will be used to illustrate the procedure. In several different formats, 14 questions were administered to leaders in four countries. Each item was hypothesized to measure the property of social harmony. For example, one of the items was: "It is desirable in reaching political decisions to reconcile as many conflicting interests as possible." Of these 14 common

[5] Stefan Nowak, "Correlational Approach to the Control of Meaning of Attitudinal Variables in Cross-Cultural Surveys," *Polish Sociological Bulletin*, 5-6, 1962.

[6] This example is taken from Adam Przeworski and Henry Teune, "Establishing Equivalence in Cross-National Research," *Public Opinion Quarterly*, 30, 1966–67.

items, four correlated in the pooled analysis (mean interitem correlation of .25) and correlated reasonably well in each system (mean interitem correlations: India, .18; Poland, .29; United States, .27; Yugoslavia, .15). Because these four items were too few to produce a satisfactory level of reliability within each country, the scales were lengthened by adding those items that best correlated with cross-national identity set in each country. By adding nation-specific items, the mean interitem correlation was reduced in three countries and and increased in one. However, the reliability of all scales was improved. Although the scales were constructed from both identical and system-specific items, the reliability of the scales based on indicators hypothesized to be related to the underlying value dimension in all countries was sufficient to produce equivalent measurement statements. In a subsequent pretest, the indicators were hypothesized in terms of characteristics of each country and the general reliability, hence the equivalence of measurement statements, improved.

In many large-scale research efforts some indicators are modified to fit glaring differences among systems. Frequently there are only judgmental criteria that measurement statements resulting from several translations of questionnaires meet the criteria of a standard language. It is possible to make a rough judgment about the equivalence of a measurement instrument despite the fact that some indicators are modified or system-specific. If there is a large number of indicators in the first place, such a judgment need only be approximate. Inkeles and Smith used the criterion of the similarity of the behavior of indicators within systems to judge the equivalence of their measure of modernity in six countries. About 150 items, incorporating 33 themes, indicating overall modernity (the OM Scale), were used to develop an instrument relative to each country. Most items were common for all countries, but some were modified for particular countries. The scores for individuals were based on the median response to all questions within each country, and the intercorrelations among the questions were examined. Inkeles and Smith concluded that "it is notable in the highest degree that a pool of some 119 attitude questions and some 40 related informational and behavioral items should show such extraordinarily similar structure in six such diverse countries. . . . It strongly suggests that man everywhere has the same structural mechanism underlying his sociopsychic functioning, despite the enormous variability of the cultural content which he embodies." [7]

[7] D. H. Smith and Alex Inkeles, "The OM Scale: A Comparative Socio-Psychological measure of Individual Modernity," *Sociometry,* **29,** 1966, p. 377.

System-Specific Indicators Only

Searching for common indicators is a conservative strategy. Adding some specific-system indicators, but only when technically necessary, is a conservative position with a concession to reality. But common indicators do not assure validity or equivalence, although they permit an additional check on cross-system reliability in a pooled analysis. Indeed, we have argued that it is generally simpler to develop measurement instruments if the indicators are initially conceptualized in system-specific terms rather than in system-free terms. The presumption in favor of the "equivalence value" of common indicators may not justify the effort of establishing their identity. In any event measurement based on indicators that are produced by the systems themselves—published data or political events—can almost never be defined in a common language. On the contrary, the language of measurement is often so different that most translations across languages is often a matter of approximation. If we are to use these important data in comparative research, we must develop procedures to evaluate the equivalence of measures based entirely on system-specific indicators. We will discuss three versions of a procedure to establish the equivalence of measurement statements based on measuring instruments composed of entirely different indicators. Since the criteria of equivalence in these procedures vary in their stringency, we shall refer to these versions as "weak" or "strong" structural criteria of equivalence.

The weakest version requires that the specific indicators have the same level of reliability in each system. In practice what would be done is to incorrelate the indicators within each system and select those that are most reliable. The system in which the indicators have the highest level of reliability would then become the standard for evaluating the equivalence of the measurement statements in the other systems. It would, of course, be desirable if the level of reliability of the set of indicators were the same (and high) across all systems. But this is not likely to happen. Even though some indicators of social harmony discussed above were common, the basic criterion of equivalence was similarly in the reliability of the indicators within each system. This procedure for establishing equivalence is based on the most obvious pattern of interrelations—mutual interdependence in the entire set of indicators. The test is weak since the hypothesis states that if all indicators are generally interrelated, the instruments are equivalent.

A stronger version of the procedure for establishing equivalence would be based on an assumption that the general properties under consideration are multidimensional. This assumption would further list the indicators appropriate for each system and would state which indicators belong to which dimension. If the general property is X, the assumption may distinguish two subdimensions, X_a and X_b and in each country specific indicators would be ordered into subdimensions, so that x^*_{a1} would be expected to belong to the dimension a in the first country, and x^{**}_{b2} would belong to the second dimension b, and so forth. Then the test of equivalence is whether factor analysis resulted in the hypothesized dimensions (with similar angles among factors) and whether specific indicators loaded in the expected manner. The instrument is based on a set of weighted indicators that can be aggregated into scores (factor scores).

An example of this kind of measurement in comparative research is the measurement of the "activeness" of local political units in the International Studies of Values in Politics. The purpose was to obtain equivalent measures of activeness in four countries. It was hypothesized that activeness had a dimension of the popular involvement of individuals in the collective life of their communities and a dimension of mobilization of resources by the political unit for collective purposes. It was anticipated that the measure of activeness, reflected by the system-specific indicators, would be a combination of indicators of popular involvement and resource mobilization and that, additionally, there would be two separate identifiable dimensions of popular involvement and resource mobilization. Although the indicators ranged from governmental expenditures, voting, and YMCA activity in the United States to smallpox vaccinations and the construction of latrines in India, a general dimension of activeness comprised of these two sets of indicators was found in each of the four countries. In one of the largest factors in each country, the predicted loadings for activeness were better than 78% of all loadings. Although the dimensions of popular involvement and resource mobilization were identifiable, they were not equally clear across all countries. An inference about the equivalence of the measures is based both on predictions of the nature of the clusters of indicators and on the "membership" of indicators in specific clusters. Because the structure of clusters is similar across systems, it can be inferred that measurement statements based on these indicators are equivalent across systems. Heterogeneous indicators are treated as components of a measure of the dimensions confirmed through factor analysis.[8]

Another example of this procedure for establishing equivalence is the research of Charles Osgood and his associates with the "semantic differen-

[8] For a discussion of this procedure with data from India and the United States, see Henry Teune, "Measurement in Comparative Research," *Comparative Political Studies,* **1**, 1968.

tial."[9] By examining "qualifying" responses, such as "merciful-cruel," "good-bad," "happy-sad," to large samples of object and property concepts, such as "sleep," "stone," "rope," and "pain," three dimensions of "qualifying experience" appeared in the orthogonal ((independent) factors across several cultures. These dimensions are called the "evaluative" factor ("good-bad," "kind-cruel"), the "potency" factor "strong-weak," "hard-soft") and the "activity" factor ("hot-cold," "fast-slow"). Although these dimensions were not initially hypothesized to be present, the fact that the structure of interrelations among the indicators appeared invariant across cultures provided a basis for inferring that measurement statements based on heterogeneous indicators were equivalent when structured according to the identified dimensions. The criterion for inferring the equivalence of measurement statements is the similarity in the structure of the indicators. The indicators, structured into these clusters by the factor loadings, compose the measurement instruments.

These measurement instruments, providing equivalent measurement statements across cultures, make it possible to seek explanations of particular scores, individual differences on "evaluation," "potency," and "activity." As long as intrasystem scores are used for explanations of relationships within systems rather than for comparison of populations across systems, it is possible to talk about the same properties for all cultures in which this structure of individual responses was found.

In the examples of the semantic differential and the measurement of community activeness, equivalence was established by a judgment about the similarity of the entire factor structure in each system. In the assessment of activeness it was possible to express how well the factors conformed to the hypothesized dimensions. However, we have only an overall measure of the similarity of the structure rather than a precise statement of the similarity, not only of the factor structures, but of each indicator in those structures. The strongest version of assessing the similarity of structures of indicators is based not only on the overall similarity of factor structures but also on an examination of the similarity of the behavior of each indicator in those structures.

In the strongest version we hypothesize that in Poland an indicator of popular participation is x, and in Chile an equivalent indicator is y. In

[9] See, for example, C. E. Osgood, "Cross-Cultural Comparability in Attitude Measurement via Multilingual Semantic Differentials," in I. Steiner and Martin Fishbein, eds., *Current Studies in Social Psychology,* Holt, Rinehart, and Winston, New York, 1965, pp. 93–107. There are several publications reporting research using the semantic differential. The logic of this approach is discussed in C. E. Osgood, G. J. Suci, and P. H. Tannenbaum, *The Measurement of Meaning,* University of Illinois Press, Urbana, 1957.

this procedure the indicators would be matched across all systems, and the dimension to which the indicator belongs would be precisely stated. Thus x and y not only indicate the same property in the two systems, but they also belong to the dimension of, say, institutional popular participation. We could say that belonging to a political party in Poland has the same "meaning" as voting in Chile, and both of these indicators belong to the institutional dimension of political participation. If there is a precise set of statements on the one-to-one correspondence of indicators and on the nature of the similarity of the dimensions of the indicators, two criteria for inferring the equivalence of measurement statements across systems become available.

The first criterion is whether the selected indicators form the factors that were predicted. This criterion is the same as that for the weaker version presented above. The second criterion is the fit of the corresponding indicators into the overall factor structure. One way of expressing this correspondence would be to correlate their factor loadings on similar factors across all systems.

What we want is a measure of the "congruence" of factor structures. Harmon suggested a familiar statistical measure—the root mean square.[10] In general it is suggested that all of the factors be compared. Various ways of expressing their congruence have been suggested.[11] In discussing the comparison of factor structures for different samples with fixed variables, Harmon concluded that "the empirical approach, employing indices of proportionality of factors, ... seems not inappropriate at this time for the 'identification' of factors across different studies." [12]

Whereas the various procedures for comparing factors across different samples assume that most of the variables are "common," or in Harmon's words "fixed," we suggest hypothesizing the correspondence of indicators even though they are not the same. This is controversial, but whether any single indicator can be considered as fixed, as indicating the same thing, under conditions of system interference is the source of the controversy, not the misapplication of statistical techniques.

Rettig and Pasamanick have published several studies showing the in-

---

[10] H. H. Harmon, *Modern Factor Analysis*, University of Chicago Press, Chicago, Rev. Ed., 1967, p. 269.

[11] The proposals for various measures of factor congruence are briefly discussed in Harmon, *ibid.*, pp. 268–71, such as the "coefficient of congruence," "degree of factorial similarity," and the "coefficient of invariance."

[12] Harmon, *ibid.*, p. 271.

variance of factor structures across heterogeneous populations.[13] However, as they assume the identity of the items in the questionnaires, they base the validity of their conclusions about invariance not only on the invariance of the factor structures, but also on the invariance of the stimuli.

Once indicators have been secured and have been shown to be interacting with each other in similar ways within each system, we can infer that we have cross-system measurement instruments. The problem, however, is that it is necessary to re-establish continuously the similarity of the structures because one of the pervasive features of the behavior of systems is that they change or at least are likely to change. Thus it could be argued that not only are measurement instruments system specific, but they are also time specific. The fact that the relationships among indicators changes over time perhaps means that we have yet another system for which new measurement instruments must be devised before comparative analysis can proceed.

Summary and Conclusions

It should be first noted that the preceding discussion was confined to the measurement of units within systems. Relationships found among indicators within systems were the basis of validating the indicators and testing their equivalence across systems. Our procedures for establishing equivalence do not extend beyond situations in which multiple indicators are available within each of several systems.

Equivalence of instruments was defined in terms of the invariance of the logical value of the measurement statements resulting from these instruments. Since we assumed throughout this discussion that direct measurement is accurate, that is, that direct measurement statements are true, the notion of the truth of inferred measurement statements was based on the concept of the validity of inferences from direct to inferred measurement statements. However, such validity cannot be tested directly since the general property being measured is not directly observable and hence does not provide a criterion. Thus an indirect way of testing validity is necessary. We proposed that such tests can be found if theoretical assumptions are made about the behavior of indicators in particular systems. Although it is a generally shared belief that the same stimuli (indicators) are more likely to provide a basis for equivalent inferences, we argued that

[13] See, for example, Solomon Rettig and Benjamin Pasamanick, "Invariance in Factor Structure of Moral Value Judgments from American and Korean College Students," *Sociometry*, **25**, 1962. The expression of invariance used on these and other populations was suggested by Y. Amhavaara.

this premise is not self-evident and is unnecessarily restrictive. Common indicators do provide a direct test of cross-system reliability. But under theoretical assumptions of varying strength, even instruments composed exclusively of indicators specific to each system can be shown to be equivalent. In the strongest version, indicators are matched across systems and their behavior with regard to hypothesized dimensions is observed. This kind of measurement clearly requires strong theoretical assumptions. But this is an advantage rather than a hindrance. Observations acquire meaning only within a theory; hence, the more explicit and the stronger the theoretical assumptions, the greater the confidence that can be placed in an instrument. Whether observations are being made or relationships are being tested, theory logically comes before research activity.

IMPLICATIONS FOR COMPARATIVE RESEARCH

The central concern of this book is the role of social systems in the development of social science theories. In the context of theory, names of systems are interpreted as residua of variables—that which is not accounted for by a theory. Within the context of measurement, systems are interpreted as determinants of the validity of inferences leading to measurement statements. The implications of these positions are that specific systems are treated as labels for unspecified factors rather than as limits of generality and that equivalence of measurement statements is treated as a matter of the validity of inferences rather than of the nature of the indicators. In order to develop theories about social systems—that is, to study them generally or comparatively—it is necessary to observe phenomena within systems. Only then is it possible to incorporate system-level variables into general theories and to establish equivalence of measurement statements.

The importance of these positions has to be viewed in terms of their implications for the conduct of comparative research. We believe that the primary implication is the shift of emphasis from data to theory. This will mean a concern for the development of theories through the exchange of findings on common theoretical problems rather than a concern for exchanging data.

A distinctive characteristic of much of the communications among social scientists in comparative research is the emphasis on the use of identical instruments and on the exchange of data for "pooled" analysis. We think the reason for so much absorption of money, time, and research facilities in the technicalities of exchanging data is the view that comparative research means to examine centrally identical data from different systems rather than build and test general theories.

A relationship between variables within a particular system can be interpreted in one of two ways: as confirmation of a hypothesis or as a finding about the system in which the relationship was observed. When any variables are observed, they are to some extent isolated from the context in which they are embedded. The concept of a "laboratory" connotes that observations made within it are largely environment free. In contrast, the concept of a "system" is that the observations are highly dependent on the system itself. Laboratory findings are usually interpreted as confirmation of general relationships. Social science findings are almost always interpreted as findings about systems.

A finding from a single laboratory or a single system constitutes evidence confirming a general statement. It is desirable to have additional confirmations from other laboratories or systems. Confirmation of a finding in another laboratory is usually treated as evidence of its generality rather than as information about the nature of laboratories around the world. Indeed every finding from different environments that confirms a general statement provides evidence for its generality. A problem arises when findings from two social systems or two laboratories differ. It is unimportant whether these findings were produced by a single research team or by independent researchers.

When findings differ, the question is why. The obvious first consideration is that the differences are due to errors in some of the observations. If there are no obvious errors, the issue is the equivalence of measurement. The cooperation of scientists is important in settling the issue of equivalence. Was the finding in one laboratory equivalent to what was found in the other? In order to begin to answer this question we can hold constant, at least mentally, certain distinctive properties of the systems or the laboratories. Detailed information can be exchanged about the nature of the measurement procedures. It may be possible to adjust the findings according to some factors known to affect the observations. But the critical question is the inferences used in measurement, not the type of indicators. This directs the problem of stimulus or indicator equivalence to the question of the equivalence of inferences and the validity of measurement statements.

But if the findings are different even after controlling for factors that may have introduced error into measurement, we have a theoretical problem. At this point the parallel between the laboratory and the system situations stops. A difference between the laboratory situation and the natural observations in the social sciences is that the former is presumed to minimize system effects in observations; the latter is presumed to exaggerate them. Because of this conception of a laboratory and its physical representation, natural scientists will most likely continue on the route of trying to locate the source of error, the extraneous variation that is uncontrolled and influences the experimental variation. Because of the conception of a social system, social scientists will expect that, in addition to variables considered by a particular theory, other factors influence the phenomena being explained. One possible solution is to conclude that "systems differ." But the position we have taken is that, if systems differ, we must search for the system-level variables that create these differences and continue to do so until all empirical remedies are exhausted.

What is important in comparative research is the exchange of findings— replicative testing of the same theories in varying social contexts. When the findings are similar, evidence accumulates to support their generality. From time to time, this evidence can be systematically evaluated. When findings are different, we need to explain those differences. The first step is to test the "equivalence" of measurement statements. If this attempt to account for differences fails, what we need to do is control for theoretically significant system-level differences that can be expressed as variables.

This focus on the exchange of findings is especially important for the conduct of cross-national research. International comparative research could proceed without the difficulties of transporting data, translating documents, recoding data into a single format, or risking disclosure of information about specific individuals or organizations to the political advantage of some governments or groups. Cross-national research could become more of a joint intellectual venture and less of an entrepreneurial task. The organization of research could be directed to a process of inquiry in which the topic of discourse would be theories, and the goal would be the increased generality of knowledge about the social world.

Selected Bibliography*

I. METHODOLOGICAL PROBLEMS AND APPROACHES

A. GENERAL PROBLEMS OF COMPARATIVE INQUIRY

Ackerknecht, E. H. "On the Comparative Method in Anthropology," in R. F. Spencer, ed., *Method and Perspective in Anthropology*. Minneapolis: University of Minnesota Press, 1954.

Bendix, Reinhard. "Concepts and Generalizations in Comparative Sociological Studies," *American Sociological Review*, **28,** 1963.

Eulau, Heinz. "Comparative Political Analysis: A Methodological Note," *Midwest Journal of Political Science*, **6,** 1962.

Ford, C. S. "On the Analysis of Behavior for Cross-Cultural Comparisons," *Behavior Science Notes*, **1,** 1966.

————, ed. *Cross-Cultural Approaches: Readings in Comparative Research*. New York: Taplinger Publishing, 1967.

Galtung, Johan. "Some Aspects of Comparative Research," *Polls*, **2,** 1967.

Gould, Julius. "Comparative Method," in J. Gould and W. L. Kolb, eds., *A Dictionary of the Social Sciences*. New York: Free Press, 1964.

Haas, Michael. "Comparative Analysis," *Western Political Quarterly*, **15,** 1962.

Haley, Jay. "Cross-Cultural Experimentation: An Initial Attempt," *Human Organization*, **26,** 1967.

Hudson, B. B., Barakat, M. K.; and Laforge, Rolfe. "Problems and Methods of Cross-cultural Research," *Journal of Social Issues*, **15,** 1959.

Lundsedt, Sven. "An Introduction to Some Evolving Problems in Cross-Cultural Research," *Journal of Social Issues*, **19,** 1963.

Marsh, R. M. "The Bearing of Comparative Analysis on Sociological Theory," *Social Forces*, **42,** 1964.

---

* For an extensive and annotated bibliography on comparative studies, see R. M. Marsh, *Comparative Sociology*. Harcourt, Brace & World, New York, 1967. The bibliography contains more than 1100 items published from 1950 to 1963.

Merritt, R. L., and Rokkan, Stein, eds. *Comparing Nations: The Use of Quantitative Data in Cross-National Research.* New Haven,: Yale University Press, 1966.

Moore, F. W., ed. *Readings in Cross-Cultural Methodology.* New Haven,: Hraf Press, 1961.

Murdock, G. P. "Feasibility and Implementation of Comparative Community Research," *American Sociological Review,* **15,** 1950.

Naroll, Raoul. "Galton's Problem: The Logic of Cross-Cultural Analysis," *Social Research,* **32,** 1965.

————. "Some Thoughts on Comparative Method in Cultural Anthropology," in H. M. Blalock and A. B. Blalock, eds., *Methodology in Social Research.* New York: McGraw-Hill, 1968.

Nowak, Stefan. "General Laws and Historical Generalizations in the Social Sciences," *Polish Sociological Bulletin,* **1,** 1961.

Radcliffe-Brown, A. R. "The Comparative Method in Anthropology," *J. Rey. Anthropology Institute of Great Britain and Ireland,* **81,** 1951.

Rokkan, Stein. "The Development of Cross-National Comparative Research: A Review of Current Problems and Possibilities," *Social Science Information,* **1,** 1962.

Scarrow, H. A. "The Scope of Comparative Analysis," *Journal of Politics,* **25,** 1963.

Scheuch, E. K. "Society as Content in Cross-National Research," *Social Science Information,* **6,** 1967.

Sjoberg, Gideon. "The Comparative Method in the Social Sciences," *Philosophy of Science,* **22,** 1955.

Smelser, N. J. "Notes on the Methodology of Comparative Analysis of Economic Activity," *Social Science Information* **6,** 1967.

Strodtbeck, F. L. "Consideraions of Meta-Method in Cross-Cultural Studies," *American Anthropologist,* **66,** Part Z—Special Publication, 1964.

Suchman, E. A. "The Comparative Method in Social Research," *Rural Sociology,* **29,** 1964.

"Summary of a Conference Discussion on Cross-Cultural Research," *Behavior Science Notes,* **2,** 1967.

Whiting, J. W. M. "Methods and Problems in Cross-Cultural Research," in G. Lindzey and E. Aronson, eds., *Handbook of Social Psychology.* Vol. II. Reading, Mass.: Addison-Wesley, 1968.

Van Nieuwenhuijze, C. A. O. *Cross-Cultural Studies.* The Hague: Mouton and Co. 1963

Verba, Sidney. "Some Dilemmas in Comparative Research," *World Politics,* **20,** 1967.

B. COMPARATIVE APPROACHES TO SPECIFIC FIELDS AND PROBLEMS

Anderson, C. A. "Methodology of Comparative Education," *International Review of Education,* **7,** 1961.

Andreski, Stanislav. *The Uses of Comparative Sociology.* Berkeley: University of California Press, 1965.

Apter, D. E. *Some Conceptual Approaches to the Study of Modernization.* Englewood Cliffs, N.J.: Prentice-Hall, 1968.

Berrol, Edward, and Holmes, Olive. "Survey and Area Approaches to International Communication Research," *Public Opinion Quarterly,* **16,** 1962.

Clark, T. N., ed. *Communiy Structure and Decision-Making: Comparative Analysis.* San Francisco: Chandler Publishing, 1968.

Farber, M. L., ed. "New Directions in the Study of National Character," *Journal of Social Issues,* **12,** 1955.

Harrison, Roger, and Hopkins, R. L. "The Design of Cross-Cultural Training: An Alternative to the University Model," *The Journal of Applied Behavioral Science,* **3,** 1967.

Henderson, N. B. "Cross-Cultural Action Research: Some Limitations, Advantages, and Problems," *Journal of Social Psychology,* **73,** 1967.

Hill, Reuben. "Cross-National Family Research: Attempts and Prospects," *International Social Science Journal,* **14,** 1962.

Inkeles, Alex and Levinson, D. J. "National Character: The Study of Modal Personality and Sociocultural Systems," in G. Lindzey, ed., *Handbook of Social Psychology.* Vol. IV. Reading, Mass.: Addison-Wesley, 1954.

Jacobson, Eugene. "Sojourn Research: A Definition of the Field," *Journal of Social Issues,* **19,** 1963.

Kim, Y. C. "The Concept of Political Culture in Comparative Politics," *Journal of Politics,* **26,** 1964.

Lasswell, H. D., and Lerner, Daniel, eds., *World Revolutionary Elites: Studies in Coercive Ideological Movements.* Cambridge,: M.I.T. Press, 1965.

Macridis, R. C. *The Comparative Study of Politics.* New York: Random House, 1955.

Martz, J. D. "The Place of Latin America in the Study of Comparative Politics," *Journal of Politics,* **28,** 1966.

Moore, W. E. "Social Change and Comparative Studies," *International Social Science Journal,* **15,** 1963.

Mukherjee, P. K. *Economic Surveys in Under-Developed Countries: A Study in Methodology.* Bombay: Asia Publishing House, 1959.

Rokkan, Stein. "The Comparative Study of Political Participation: Notes Toward a Perspective on Current Research," in A. Ranney, ed., *Essays on the Behavioral Study of Politics.* Urbana: University of Illinois Press, 1962.

Scarrow, H. A. *Comparative Political Analysis.* New York: Harper & Row, 1969.

Shoup, Paul. "Comparing Communist Nations: Prospects for an Empirical Approach," *American Political Science Review,* **62,** 1968.

Stone, I. T. "An Approach to the Comparative Study of Social Integration," *American Anthropologist,* **66,** 1964.

C. GENERAL METHODOLOGICAL PROBLEMS

Driver, H. E. "Introduction to Statistics for Comparative Research," in F. W. Moore, ed., *Readings in Cross-Cultural Methodology.* New Haven, Conn.: Hraf Press, 1961.

Eggan, F. R. "Social Anthropology and the Method of Controlled Comparison," *American Anthropologist,* **56,** 1954.

Evan, W. M. "Cohort Analysis of Survey Data: A Procedure for Studying Long-Term Opinion Change," *Public Opinion Quarterly,* **23,** 1959.

Hendriksen, P. M. "Methodological Aspects of NRU/NTS Continuous Program Research," *Polls,* **2,** 1967.

Moore, F. W. "Sampling Utilized in 50 Cross-Cultural Studies," *Behavior Science Notes,* **2,** 1967.

Murdock, G. P. "World Ethnographic Sample," *American Anthropologist,* **59,** 1957.

Naroll, Raoul. "Two Solutions to Galton's Problem," *Philosophy of Science,* **28,** 1961.

Naroll, Raoul, and D'Andrade, R. G. "Two Further Solutions to Galton's Problem," *American Anthropologist,* **65,** 1963.

Naroll, Raoul. "A Fifth Solution to Galton's Problem," *American Anthropologist,* **66,** 1964.

Rokkan, Stein. "Archives for Secondary Analysis of Sample Survey Data: An Early Inquiry into the Prospects for Western Europe." *International Social Science Journal,* **16,** 1964.

————. "The Comparative Study of Electoral Statistics: An Introductory Note," *Social Sciences Information,* **5,** 1966.

Stern, Eric. "Comparing Results from Different Cultures," *International Social Science Bulletin,* **5,** 1953.

Zelditch, Morris, Jr. "Some Methodological Problems of Field Studies," *American Journal of Sociology,* **68,** 1962.

D. METHODOLOGICAL PROBLEMS OF ATTITUDE MEASUREMENT

Abu-Lughod, Ibrahim. "International News in the Arabic Press: A Comparative Content Analysis," *Public Opinion Quarterly,* **26,** 1962.

Anderson, Bo; Zelditch, Morris; Takagi, Paul; and Whiteside, Don. "On Conservative Attitudes," *Acta Sociologica,* **8,** 1964.

Brouwer, Marten. "The 1963 Production of Sample Surveys in Continental Europe," *Social Sciences Information,* **4,** 1965.

Bruce, W., and Anderson, R. "On the Comparability of Meaningful Stimuli in Cross-Cultural Research," *Sociometry,* **30,** 1967.

Converse, P. E. "New Dimensions of Meaning for Cross-Section Sample Surveys in Politics," *International Social Science Journal,* **16,** 1964.

Duijker, H. C. J. "Comparative Research in Social Science with Special Reference to Attitude Research," *International Social Science Bulletin,* **7,** 1955.

Hoffmann, Michel. "Research on Opinions and Attitudes in West Africa," *International Social Science Journal,* **15,** 1963.

Jacobson, Eugene. "Methods Used for Producing Comparable Data in the OCSR Seven-Nation Attitude Study," *Journal of Social Issues,* **10,** 1954.

Jacobson, Eugene; Kumata, Hideya; and Gullahorn, J. E. "Cross-Cultural Contributions to Attitude Research," *Public Opinion Quarterly,* **24,** 1960.

Kapferer, Clodwig. "The Use of Sample Surveys by OECD," *International Social Science Journal,* **16,** 1964.

Kaplan, Bert, ed. *Studying Personality Cross-Culturally.* Evanston, Ill.: Row Peterson, 1961.

McClintock, C. G., and McNeel, S. P. "Cross-Cultural Comparisons of Interpersonal Motives," *Sociometry,* **29,** 1966.

Michael, D. N. "The Use of Culture Concepts in the Functional Analysis of Public Opinion," *International Journal of Opinion and Attitude Research,* **5,** 1951.

Nowak, Stefan. "Correlational Approach to the Control of Meaning of Attitudinal Variables in Cross-Cultural Surveys," *Polish Sociological Bulletin,* **5–6,** 1962.

Osgood, C. E. "On the Strategy of Cross-National Research into Subjective Culture," *Social Science Information,* **6,** 1967.

———. "The Cross-Cultural Generality of Visual-Verbal Synethestic Tendencies," *Behavioral Science,* **5,** 1960.

Pool, Ithiel de Sola. "Use of Available Sample Surveys in Comparative Research," *Social Sciences Information,* **2,** 1963.

Pool, Ithiel de Sola, and Abelson, R. P. "The Simulatics Project," *Public Opinion Quarterly,* **25,** 1961.

Przeworski, Adam, and Teune, Henry. "Establishing Equivalence in Cross-National Research," *Public Opinion Quarterly,* **30,** 1966.

Rokkan, Stein. "The Use of Sample Surveys in Comparative Research," *International Social Science Journal,* **16,** 1964.

Rommetneit, Ragnar, and Israel, Joachim. "Notes on the Standardization of Experimental Manipulations and Measurements in Cross-National Research," *Journal of Social Issues,* **10,** 1954.

Sebald, Hans. "Studying National Character through Comparative Content Analysis," *Social Forces,* **40,** 1962.

Stapel, Jan. "Results and Problems of International Polling," *International Social Science Bulletin,* **5,** 1953.

Suchman, E. A. "Public Opinion Research Across National Boundaries," *Public Opinion Quarterly,* **22,** 1958.

Wilson, E. C. "Adapting Probability Sampling to Western Europe," *Public Opinion Quarterly,* **14,** 1950.

———. "World-Wide Development of Opinion Research," *Public Opinion Quarterly,* **21,** 1957.

F. METHODOLOGICAL PROBLEMS OF AGGREGATE DATA RESEARCH

Alker, H. R. "The Comparison of Aggregate Political and Social Data: Potentialities and Problems," *Social Science Information,* **5,** 1966.

Gold, David. "Some Problems in Generalizing Aggregate Associations," *American Behavioral Scientist,* **8,** 1964.

Gibbs, F. P. "Measures of Urbanization," *Social Forces,* **45,** 1966; and Comment by F. L. Jones, **46,** 1967.

Ramsey, C. E., and Collazo, Jenaro. "Some Problems of Cross-Cultural Measurement," *Rural Sociology,* **25,** 1960.

Retzlaff, R. H. "The Use of Aggregate Data in Comparative Political Analysis," *Journal of Politics,* **27,** 1965.

Runciman, W. G. "A Method for Cross-National Comparison of Political Consensus," *British Journal of Sociology,* **13,** 1962.

Teune, Henry. "Measurement in Comparative Research," *Comparative Political Studies,* **1,** 1968.

F. ERRORS OF MEASUREMENT AND FIELD PROBLEMS

Back, K. W. and Stycos, J. M. *The Survey Under Unusual Conditions: Methodological Facets of the Jamaica Human Fertility Investigation.* Ithaca, N.Y.: Society for Applied Anthropology, 1959.

Bonilla, Frank. "Elites and Public Opinion in Areas of High Social Stratification," *Public Opinion Quarterly,* **22,** 1958.

Carter, R. E., Jr. "Some Problems and Distinctions in Cross-Cultural Research," *American Behavioral Scientist,* **9,** 1966.

Doob, L. W. "The Use of Different Test Items in Nonliterate Societies," *Public Opinion Quarterly,* **21,** 1957.

Erwin, S. M. "Language and TAT Content in Bilinguals," *Journal of Abnormal and Social Psychology,* **60,** 1964.

Erwin, S. M., and Bower, R. T. "Translation Problems in International Surveys," *Public Opinion Quarterly,* **16,** 1952.

Fink, R. "Interviewer Training and Supervision in a Survey of Laos," *International Social Science Journal,* **15,** 1963.

Frey, F. W. "Surveying Peasant Attitudes in Turkey," *Public Opinion Quarterly,* **27,** 1963.

Hunt, W. H.; Crane, W. W.; and Wahlke, J. C. "Interviewing Political Elites in Cross-Cultural Comparative Research," *American Journal of Sociology,* **70,** 1964.

Jones, A. G. "The Survey Method in Under-developed Areas," *International Social Science Bulletin,* **5,** 1953.

Jones, E. L. "The Courtesy Bias in South-East Asian Surveys," *International Social Science Journal,* **15,** 1963.

Landsberger, H. A., and Saavedra, Antonio. "Response Set in Developing Countries," *Public Opinion Quarterly,* **31,** 1967.

Lerner, Daniel. "Interviewing European Elites," *Polls,* **2,** 1966.

Mukherjee, B. N., and Verma, Sitapai. "A Cross-Cultural Comparison of Judgments of Social Desirability for Items of a Force-Choice Scale of Achievement Motivation," *Journal of Social Psychology,* **69,** 1966.

Naroll, Raoul. *Data Quality Control—A New Research Technique: Prolegomena to a Cross-Cultural Study of Culture Stress.* New York: Free Press, 1962.

Phillips, H. P. "Problems of Translation and Meaning in Field Work," *Human Organization,* **18,** 1959–60.

Schachter, Stanley. "Interpretive and Methodological Problems of Replicated Research," *Journal of Social Issues,* **10,** 1954.

Steetzel, Jean. *Jeunesse sans Chrysantheme ni sabre.* Paris: Plon-UNESCO, 1954.

Stycos, J. M. "Interviewer Training in Another Culture," *Public Opinion Quarterly,* **16,** 1952.

Ward, R. E. *Studying Politics Abroad.* Boston: Little, Brown, 1964.

Wilson, E. C. "Problems of Survey Research in Modernizing Areas," *Public Opinion Quarterly,* **22,** 1958.

G. SPECIFIC ATTITUDE INSTRUMENTS

Adcock, C. J., and Ritchie, J. E. "Intercultural Use of Rorschach," *American Anthropologist,* **60,** 1958.

Antler, Lawrence; Zaretsky, H. N.; and Ritter, Walter. "The Practical Validity of the Gordon Personal Profile Among United States and Foreign Medical Residents," *Journal of Social Psychology,* **72,** 1967.

Cantril, Hadley, and Free, L. A. "Hopes and Fears for Self and Country: The Self-Anchoring Scale in Cross-Cultural Research," *American Behavioral Scientist,* **6,** 1962.

Ghei, S. N. "The Reliability and Validity of Edwards Personal Preference Schedule: A Cross-Cultural Study," *Journal of Social Psychology,* **61,** 1963.

Gordon, L. V., and Kikuchi, Akio. "American Personality Tests in Cross-Cultural Research—A Caution," *Journal of Social Psychology,* **69,** 1966.

Kikuchi, Akio, and Gordon, L. V. "Evaluation and Cross-Cultural Application of a Japanese Form of the Survey of Interpersonal Values," *Journal of Social Psychology,* **69,** 1966.

Lindzey, Gardner. *Projective Techniques and Cross-Cultural Research.* New York: Appleton-Century-Crofts, 1961.

Melikian, L. H. "The Use of Selected T.A.T. Cards Among Arab University Students: A Cross-Cultural Study," *Journal of Social Psychology,* **62,** 1964.

Osgood, C. E. "Semantic Differential Technique in the Comparative Study of Cultures," *American Anthropologist,* **66,** 1964.

Rabin, A. I., and Limuaco, J. A. "A Comparison of the Connotative Meaning of Rorschach's Inkblots for American and Filipino Students," *Journal of Social Psychology,* **72,** 1967.

Rose, E., and Willoughby, G. "Culture Profiles and Emphases," *American Journal of Sociology,* **63,** 1958.

Sundberg, N. D. "The Use of the MMPI for Cross-Culture Personality Study: A Preliminary Report on the German Translator," *Journal of Abnormal and Social Psychology,* **52,** 1956.

Yamamura, D. S., and Zald, M. N. "A Note on the Usefulness and Validity of the Herbst Family Questionnaires," *Human Relations,* **9,** 1956.

II. CROSS-NATIONAL AND CROSS-CULTURAL STUDIES

A. POLITICAL ATTITUDES

Almond, G. A. and Verba, Sidney. *The Civic Culture: Political Attitudes and Democracy in Five Nations.* Princeton, N.J.: Princeton University Press, 1963.

Bonilla, Frank. *A Comparative Study of the Audience for Mass Media in Three Latin American Capitals.* New York: Columbia University Press, 1953.

Cantril, Hadley. *The Politics of Despair.* New York: Basic Books, 1958.

Cantril, Hadley, and Strunk, Mildred, eds. *Public Opinion 1935–1946.* Princeton, N.J.: Princeton University Press, 1951.

Converse, P. E., and Dupeux, Georges. "Politicization of the Electorate in France and the United States," *Public Opinion Quarterly,* **26,** 1962.

Dodd, S. C., et al. *A Pioneer Radio Poll in Lebanon, Syria, and Palestine.* Palestine Government Printer, 1943.

Free, L. A. *Six Allies and A Neutral.* New York: Free Press, 1959.

Galtung, Johan. *Atoms for Peace: A Comparative Study of Student Attitudes.* Oslo: Institute for Social Research, 1960.

Gillespie, J. M., and Allport, G. W. *Youth's Outlook on the Future: A Cross-National Study.* New York: Doubleday, 1955.

Kornberg, Allan, and Thomas, Norman. "The Political Socialization of National Legislative Elites in the United States and Canada," *Journal of Politics,* **27,** 1965.

Kuroda, Yasumasa. "A Cross-Cultural Analysis of the Desire for Political Power: Empirical Findings and Theoretical Implications," *Western Political Quarterly,* **20,** 1967.

Moskos, C. C., and Bell, Wendell. "Attitudes Towards Democracy Among Leaders in Four Emergent Nations," *British Journal of Sociology,* **15,** 1964.

Rokkan, Stein. "Party Preferences and Opinion Patterns in Western Europe: A Comparative Analysis," *International Social Science Bulletin,* **7,** 1955.

B. ACHIEVEMENT AND MODERNITY

Doob, L. W. *Becoming More Civilized: A Psychological Interpretation.* New Haven,: Yale University Press, 1960.

Joshi, Vidya. "Personality Profiles in Industrial and Preindustrial Cultures: A TAT Study," *Journal of Social Psychology,* **66,** 1965.

Kahl, J. A. "Modern Values and Fertility Ideals in Brazil and Mexico," *Journal of Social Issues,* **23,** 1967.

———. "Some Measurement of Achievement Orientation," *American Journal of Sociology,* **70,** 1965.

———. *The Measurement of Modernism, A Study of Values in Brazil and Mexico.* Austin: University of Texas, 1968.

Lerner, David. *The Passing of Traditional Society: Modernizing the Middle East.* Glencoe, Ill.: Free Press, 1958.

McClelland, D. C. "Motivational Patterns in Southeast Asia with Special Reference to the Chinese Case," *Journal of Social Issues,* **19,** 1963.

———. *The Achieving Society.* Princeton, N.J.: D. Van Nostrand, 1961.

Pearlin, L. I., and Kohn, M. L. "Social Class, Occupation, and Parental Values: A Cross-National Study," *American Sociological Review*, **31**, 1966.

Smith, D. H., and Inkeles, Alex. "The OM Scale: A Comparative Socio-Psychological Measure of Individual Modernity," *Sociometry*, **29**, 1966.

Tedeschi, J. T., and Kian, Mohamed. "Cross-Cultural Study of the T.A.T. Assessment for Achievement Motivation: Americans and Persians," *Journal of Social Psychology*, **58**, 1962.

C. AUTHORITARIANISM

Arkoff, Abe; Meredith, Gerald; and Iwahara, Shinkuro. "Male Dominant and Equalitarian Attitudes in Japanaese, Japanese-American and Caucasian-American Students," *Journal of Social Psychology*, **64**, 1964.

Meade, R. D., and Whittaker, J. O. "A Cross-Cultural Study of Authoritarianism," *Journal of Social Psychology*, **72**, 1967.

Melikian, L. H. "Authoritarianism and Its Correlates in the Egyptian Culture and in the United States," *Journal of Social Issues*, **15**, 1959.

Prothro, E. T., and Melikian, L. H. "The California Public Opinion Scale in an Authoritarian Culture," *Public Opinion Quarterly*, **17**, 1953.

Sallery, R. D. H., and Lindgren, H. C. "Arab Attitudes Toward Authority: A Cross-Cultural Study," *Journal of Social Psychology*, **69**, 1966

D. SOCIAL STEREOTYPES AND SOCIAL DISTANCE

Bogardus, E. S. "Comparing Racial Distance in Ethiopia, South Africa, and the United States," *Sociology and Social Research*, **52**, 1968.

Brunar, J. S., and Perlmutter, H. V. "Compatriot and Foreigner: A Study of Impression Formation in Three Countries," *Journal of Abnormal and Social Psychology*, **55**, 1957.

Buchanan, William, and Cantril, Hadley. *How Nations See Each Other: A Study in Public Opinion*. Urbana: University of Illinois Press, 1953.

Duijker, H. C. J., and Frijda, N. H. *National Character and National Stereotypes*. New York: Humanities Press, 1960.

Gullahorn, J. E., and Loomis, C. E. "A Comparison of Social Distance Attitudes in the United States and Mexico," *Studies in Comparative International Development*. St. Louis: Washington University, 1966.

Lambert, W. E. "Comparisons of French and American Modes of Response to the Bogardus Social Distance Scale," *Social Forces*, **31**, 1952.

Lambert, W. E., and Klineberg, D. A. "Pilot Study of the Origin and Development of National Stereotypes," *International Social Science Journal*, **11**, 1959.

Reigstoski, Erich, and Anderson, Nels. "National Stereotypes and Foreign Contacts," *Public Opinion Quarterly*, **23**, 1959.

Triandis, H. C., and Triandis, L. M. "Race, Social Class, Religion, and Nationality as Determinants of Social Distance," *Journal of Abnormal and Social Psychology,* **61,** 1960.

E. MORAL JUDGMENTS AND VALUES

Ayal, E. B. "Value Systems and Economic Development in Japan and Thailand," *Journal of Social Issues,* **19,** 1963.

Berrien, F. K. "Japanese vs. American Values," *Journal of Social Psychology,* **65,** 1965.

Gordon, L. V., and Kakkar, S. B. "A Cross-Cultural Study of Indian and American Interpersonal Values," *Journal of Social Psychology,* **69,** 1966.

Lipset, S. M. "The Value Patterns of Democracy: A Case Study in Comparative Analysis," *American Sociological Review,* **28,** 1963.

McGrahahan, D. Y. "A Comparison of Social Attitudes among American and German Youth," *Journal of Abnormal and Social Psychology,* **41,** 1946.

Morris, Charles. *Varieties of Human Values.* Chicago: University of Chicago Press, 1956.

Rettig, Salomon. "Invariance of Factor Structure of Ethical Judgments by Indian and American College Students," *Sociometry,* **27,** 1964.

Rettig, Salomon, and Pasamanick, Benjamin. "Invariance in Factor Structure of Moral Value Judgments from American and Korean College Students," *Sociometry,* **25,** 1962.

————. "Moral Codes of American and Korean College Students," *Journal of Social Psychology,* **50,** 1959.

Singh, P. N.; Huang, S. C.; and Thompson, G. C. "A Comparative Study of Selected Attitudes, Values and Personality Characteristics of American, Chinese and Indian Students," *Journal of Social Psychology,* **57,** 1962.

Stycos, J. M. "Contraception and Catholicism in Latin America," *Journal of Social Issues,* **23,** 1967.

Tomeh, A. K. "Moral Values in a Cross-Cultural Perspective," *Journal of Social Psychology,* **74,** 1968.

F. PERSONALITY AND SOCIALIZATION

Anderson, H. H., and Anderson, G. L. "Cultural Reactions to Conflict: A Study of Adolescent Children in Seven Countries," in G. M. Gilbert, ed., *Psychological Approaches to Intergroup and International Understanding.* Austin: University of Texas, 1956.

Anderson, H. H.; Anderson, G. L.; Cohen, I. H.; Nutt, F. D. "Image of the Teacher by Adolescent Children in Four Countries: Germany, England, Mexico, and the United States," *Journal of Social Psychology,* **50,** 1959.

Barry, Herbert; Bacon, M. K.; and Child, I. L. "A Cross-Cultural Survey of Some Sex Differences in Socialization," *Journal of Abnormal and Social Psychology,* **55,** 1957.

Brown, J. K. "A Cross-Cultural Study of Female Initiation Rites," *American Anthropologist,* **65,** 1963.

Gaier, E. L., and Littemen, Y. "Modes of Conformity, in Two Sub-cultures: A Finnish-American Comparison," *Acta Sociologica*, 5, 1961.

Hallowell, A. I. "Accultination Processes and Personality Changes as Indicated by the Rorschach Technique," *Rorschach Research Exchange*, 6, 1942.

McClelland, D. C.; Sturr, J. F.; Knapp, R. H.; and Wendt, H. W. "Obligations to Self and Society in the United States and Germany," *Journal of Abnormal and Social Psychology*, 56, 1958.

Pettigrew, T. F. "Personality and Socio-Cultural Factors in Intergroup Attitudes: A Cross-National Comparison," *Journal of Conflict Resolution*, 2, 1958.

Plog, S. C. "The Disclosure of Self in the United States and Germany," *Journal of Social Psychology*, 65, 1965.

Rabin, A. I. "A Comparison of American and Israeli Children by Means of a Sentence Completion Technique," *Journal of Social Psychology*, 49, 1959.

Rabin, A. I., and Limuaco, Josefina. "Sexual Differentiation Of American and Filipino Children as Reflected in the Draw-A-Person Test," *Journal of Social Psychology*, 50, 1959.

Shirley, R. W., and Romney, A. K. "Love Magic and Socialization Anxiety: A Cross-Cultural Study," *American Anthropologist*, 64, 1962.

Stephens, W. N. *The Oedipus Complex: Cross-Cultural Evidence.* New York: Free Press, 1962.

Terhune, K. W. "An Examination of Some Contributing Demographic Variables in a Cross-National Study," *Journal of Social Psychology*, 59, 1963.

Triandis, L. M., and Lambert, W. W. "Pancultural Factor Analyses of Reported Socialization Practices," *Journal of Abnormal and Social Psychology*, 62, 1961.

Tsujioka, Bien, and Cattell, R. B. "A Cross-Cultural Comparison of Second-Stratum Questionnaire Personality Factor Structures—Anxiety and Extraversion—in America and Japan," *Journal of Social Psychology*, 65, 1965.

G. PERCEPTIONS AND OTHER BEHAVIORAL DISPOSITIONS

Allport, Gordon, and Pettigrew, Thomas. "Cultural Influence on the Perception of Movement: The Trapezoidal Illusion Among Zulus," *Journal of Abnormal and Social Psychology*, 55, 1957.

Cantril, Hadley. *Patterns of Human Concerns.* New Brunswick, N.J.: Rutgers University Press, 1965.

Hudson, B. B., ed. "Cross-Cultural Studies in the Arab Middle East and United States: Studies of Young Adults," *Journal of Social Issues*, 15, 1959.

Lindgren, H. C., and Lindgren, Fredrica. "Creativity, Brainstorming, and Orneriness: A Cross-Cultural Study," *Journal of Social Psychology*, 67, 1965.

Madaus, George. "A Cross-Cultural Comparison of the Factor Structure of Selected Tests of Divergent Thinking," *Journal of Social Psychology*, **73**, 1967.

Maclay, Howard, and Ware, E. E. "Cross-Cultural Use of the Semantic Differential," *Behavioral Science*, **6**, 1961.

McClelland, D. C. ,*et al.* "A Cross-Cultural Study of Folk-Tale Content and Drinking," *Sociometry*, **29**, 1966.

Milgram, Stanley. "Nationality and Conformity," *Scientific American*, **6**, 1961.

Nall, F. C. "Role Expectations: A Cross-Cultural Study," *Rural Sociology*, **29**, 1962.

Osgood, C. E.; Suci, G. J.; and Tannenbaum, P. H. *The Measurement of Meaning*. Urbana: University of Illinois Press, 1957.

Schuh, A. J., and Quesada, Carmencita. "Attitudes of Filipino and American College Students Assessed with the Semantic Differential," *Journal of Social Psychology*, **72**, 1967.

Segall, M. H.; Campbell, D. T.; and Herskovits, M. J. *The Influence of Culture on Visual Perception*. Indianapolis: Bobbs-Merrill, 1966.

Singh, P. N. and Rettig, Salomon. "Cross-Cultural Differences in Habitual Response Preferences as an Index of Anxiety," *Journal of Social Psychology*, **58**, 1962.

Szalay, L. B., and Brent, J. E. "The Analysis of Cultural Meanings Through Free Verbal Associations," *Journal of Social Psychology*, **72**, 1967.

Tajfel, Henri. "Social and Cultural Factors in Perception," in G. Lindzey and E. Aronson, eds. *Handbook of Social Psychology*. Vol. III. Reading, Mass.: Addison-Wesley, 1968.

Tanaka, Yasumasa. "Cross-Cultural Compatibility of the Affective Meaning Systems," *Journal of Social Issues*, **23**, 1967.

Triandis, H. C. "Cultural Influences Upon Cognitive Processes," in Leonard Berkowitz, ed. *Advances in Experimental Social Psychology*. New York: Academic Press, 1964.

————. "Some Cross-Cultural Studies of Cognitive Consistency," in R. P. Abelson, E. Aronson, W. J. McGuire, T. M. Newcomb, M. J. Rosenberg, and P. H. Tannenbaum, eds., *Theories of Cognitive Consistency: A Sourcebook*. Chicago: Rand McNally, 1968.

Watson, J. B., and Nelson, H. E. "Body Environment Transactions: A Standard Model for Cross-Cultural Analyses," *Southwestern Journal of Anthropology*, **23**, 1967.

White, J. H. "Some Attitudes of South African Nurses—A Cross-Cultural Study," *Journal of Social Psychology*, **69**, 1966.

H. INDIVIDUAL BEHAVIOR

Bacon, M. K., *et al.* "A Cross-Cultural Study of Correlates of Crime," *Journal of Abnormal and Social Psychology*, **66**, 1963.

Barry, Herbert; Child, I. L.; and Bacon, M. K. "Relation of Child Training to Subsistence Economy," *American Anthropologist*, **61**, 1959.

Clifton, J. A. "The Acceptance of External Political Controls on Truk and Ponape," *International Journal of Comparative Sociology*, **5**, 1964.

DeFleur, L. B. "Cross-Cultural Comparison of Juvenile Offenders: Cordoba, Argentina, and the United States," *Social Problems*, **14**, 1967.

Gonzalez, N. S. "Health Behavior in Cross-Cultural Perspective," *Human Organization*, **25**, 1966.

Kole, D. M. "A Cross-Cultural Study of Medical-Psychiatric Symptoms," *Journal of Health and Human Behavior*, **7**, 1966.

Lloyd, B. B. "Choice Behavior and Social Structure: A Comparison of Two African Societies," *Journal of Social Psychology*, **74**, 1968.

Montague, J., Jr. "Professionalism Among American, Australian, and English Physicians," *Journal of Health and Human Behavior*, **7**, 1966.

Otterbein, K. F., and Otterbein, C. S. "An Eye for an Eye, a Tooth for a Tooth:: A Cross-Cultural Study of Feuding," *American Anthropologist*, **67**, 1965.

Roberts, J. M., and Sutton-Smith, Brian. "Cross-Cultural Correlates of Games of Chance," *Behavior Science Notes*, **1**, 1966.

Rokkan, Stein, and Campbell, Angus. "Factors in the Recruitment of Active Participants in Politics: A Comparative Analysis of Survey Data for Norway and the United States," *International Social Science Journal*, **12**, 1960.

Rosenblatt, P. C. "Functions of Games: An Examination of Individual Difference Hypotheses Derived from a Cross-Cultural Study," *Journal of Social Psychology*, **58**, 1962.

Soddy, Kenneth, ed. *Cross-Cultural Studies in Mental Health: Identity—Mental Health and Value Systems*. Chicago: Quadrangle Books, 1962.

Sheldon, Alan, and Hopper, Douglas. "Psychiatric Care in Cross-Cultural Perspective," *Human Organization*, **25**, 1966.

Varela, J. A. "A Cross-Cultural Replication of an Experiment Involving Birth Order," *Journal of Abnormal and Social Psychology*, **69**, 1964.

Wagner, N. N. "Birth Order of Volunteers: Cross-Cultural Data," *Journal of Social Psychology*, **74**, 1968.

I. GROUPS, ORGANIZATIONS, INSTITUTIONS

Blisten, D. R. *The World of the Family: A Comparative Study of Family Organizations in their Social and Cultural Settings*. New York: Random House, 1963.

Burch, T. K. "The Size and Structure of Families: A Comparative Analysis of Census Data," *American Sociological Review*, **32**, 1967.

Georgopoulos, Basil. "Normative Structure Variables and Organizational Behavior: A Comparative Study," *Human Relations*, **18**, 1965.

LeVine, R. A. "The Role of the Family in Authority Systems: A Cross-Cultural Application of Stimulus Generalization Theory," *Behavioral Science,* **5,** 1960.

Matras, Judah. "Social Strategies of Family Formation: Some Comparative Data for Scandinavia, the British Isles and North America," *International Social Science Journal,* **17,** 1965.

Raffaele, J. A. *Labor Leadership in Italy and Denmark.* Madison: University of Wisconsin Press, 1962.

Rainwater, Lee. "Family Planning in Cross-National Perspective: An Overview," *Journal of Social Issues,* **23,** 1967.

Stephens, W. N. *The Family in Cross-Cultural Perspective.* New York: Holt, Rinehart and Winston, 1963.

Sweetser, F. L. "Factor Structure as Ecological Structure in Helsinki and Boston," *Acta Sociologica,* **8,** 1965.

Sunderland, S. C. "Changing Universities: A Cross-Cultural Approach," *Journal of Applied Behavioral Science,* **3,** 1967.

Young, F. W. "A Proposal for Cooperative Cross-Cultural Research on Intervillage Systems," *Human Organization,* **25,** 1966.

Young, F. W. and Young, R. C. "The Sequence and Direction of Community Growth: A Cross-Cultural Generalization," *Rural Sociology,* **27,** 1962.

J. SOCIAL STRUCTURE AND SOCIAL MOBILITY

Carlsson, Gosta. *Social Mobility and Class Structure.* Lund, C. W. K., Gleerup, 1958.

Cutright, Phillips. "Inequality: A Cross-National Analysis," *American Sociological Review,* **32,** 1967.

Glass, D. V., ed. *Social Mobility in Britain.* London: Routlege and Kegan Paul, 1954.

Haller, A. O., and Lewis, D. M. "The Hypothesis of Intersocietal Similarity in Occupational Prestige Hierarchies," *American Journal of Sociology,* **72,** 1962.

Haller, A. O.; Lewis, D. M.; and Ishino, Iwao. "The Hypothesis of Intersocietal Similarity in Occupational Prestige Hierarchies," *American Journal of Sociology,* **72,** 1966.

Inkeles, Alex. "Industrial Man: The Relation of Status to Experience, Perception and Value," *American Journal of Sociology,* **66,** 1960.

Lenski, Gerhard. "Status Inconsistency and the Vote: A Four Nation Test," *American Sociological Review,* **32,** 1967.

Lipset, S. M. "Research Problems in the Comparative Analysis of Mobility and Development," *International Social Science Journal,* **16,** 1964.

Lopreato, Joseph. "Upward Social Mobility and Political Orientation," *American Sociological Review,* **32,** 1967.

Lydall, H., and Launing, J. B. "A Comparison of the Distribution of Personal Income and Wealth in the United States and Great Britain," *American Economic Review,* **49,** 1959.

Marsh, R. M. "Values, Demand, and Social Mobility," *American Sociological Review,* **28,** 1963.

Matras, Judah. "Comparison of Integenerational Occupational Mobility Patterns: An Application of the Formal Theory of Social Mobility," *Population Studies,* **14,** 1960.

Miller, S. M. "Comparative Social Mobility," *Current Sociology,* **9,** 1960.

Mitchell, J. C. "Occupational Prestige and the Social System: A Problem in Comparative Sociology," *International Journal of Comparative Sociology,* **5,** 1964.

Morsbach, Helmut, and Morsbach, Gisela. "A Cross-Cultural Investigation of Occupational Stereotypes in Three South African Groups, *Journal of Social Psychology,* **73,** 1967.

Ramsey, C. E., and Smith, R. J. "Japanese and American Perceptions of Occupations," *American Journal of Sociology,* **65,** 1960.

Rogoff, N. "Social Stratification in France and the U.S.," *American Journal of Sociology,* **58,** 1953.

Runciman, W. G. "Industrial Man: The Relation of Status to Experience, Perception and Value," *American Journal of Sociology,* **66,** 1961, with a rejoinder by A. Inkeles.

Spiro, M. E. "A Typology of Social Structure and the Patterning of Social Institutions: A Cross-Cultural Study," *American Anthropologist,* **67,** 1965.

Svalastoga, Kaare. *Prestige, Class, and Mobility.* Copenhagen: Gyldendal Scandinavian University Books, 1959.

Thomas, E. M. "Reinspecting a Structural Position on Occupational Prestige," *American Journal of Sociology,* **67,** 1962.

Turner, R. H. "Acceptance of Irregular Mobility in Britain and the United States," *Sociometry,* **29,** 1966.

K. CONFLICT WITHIN AND BETWEEN NATIONS

Feierabend, I. K., and Feierabend, R. L. "Agressive Behavior Within Polities, 1948–1962: A Cross-National Study," *Journal of Conflict Resolution,* **10,** 1966.

Havens, A. E., and Potter, H. R. "Organizational and Societal Variables in Conflict Resolution," *Human Organization,* **26,** 1967.

Rummel, R. J. "Testing Some Possible Predictors of Conflict Within and Between Nations," *Peace Research Society, Papers,* **1,** 1964.

Tanter, Raymond. "Dimensions of Conflict Behavior Within Nations, 1955–60: Turmoil and Internal War," *Peace Research Society, Papers,* **3,** 1965.

L. POLITICAL PARTIES, POLITICAL DEVELOPMENT

Cutright, Phillips. "National Political Development, Measurement, and Analysis," *American Sociological Review,* **28,** 1963.

Edelman, Murray, and Fleming, R. W. *The Politics of Wage-Price Decisions: A Four Country Analysis.* Urbana: University of Illinois Press, 1965.

Etzioni, Amitai. *Political Unification; A Comparative Study of Leaders and Forces.* New York: Holt, Rinehart and Winston, 1965.

Fitzgibbon, R. H. "A Statistical Evaluation of Latin American Democracy," *Western Political Quarterly,* **9,** 1956.

Heidenheimer, A. J. "Comparative Party Finance: Notes on Practices and Toward A Theory," *Journal of Politics,* **25,** 1963.

Johnson, S. D. "A Comparative Study of Inter-Party Factionalism in Israel and Japan," *Western Political Quarterly,* **20,** 1967.

Lowell, A. L. "The Influence of Party upon Legislation in England and America," *Annual Report of the American Historical Association for 1901,* **1,** 1902.

Snow, P. G. "A Scalogram Analysis of Political Development," *American Behavioral Scientist,* **9,** 1966.

Tanter, Raymond. "Toward A Theory of Political Development," *Midwest Journal of Political Science,* **11,** 1967.

M. COUNTRY-LEVEL STUDIES

Adelman, Irma, and Morris, C. T. *Society, Politics and Economic Development.* Baltimore: Johns Hopkins Press, 1967.

Banks, A. S., and Gregg, P. M. "Grouping Political Systems: Q-Factor Analysis of a Cross-Polity Survey," *American Behavioral Scientist,* **9,** 1965.

Banks, A. S., and Textor, R. B. *A Cross-Polity Survey.* Cambridge, Mass.: M.I.T. Press, 1963.

Cattell, R. B. *et al.* "An Attempt At More Refined Definition of Cultural Dimensions of Syntality in Modern Nations," *American Sociological Review,* **17,** 1952.

Cattell, R. B., and Gersuch, R. M. "The Definition and Measurement of National Morale and Morality," *Journal of Social Psychology,* **67,** 1965.

Corneliss, P. A. "The Volume of East-West Trade," *Coexistence,* **2,** 1964.

Cutright, Phillips. "Income Redistribution:: A Cross-National Analysis," *Social Forces,* **46,** 1967.

Eitzen, D. S. "The Use of Bank's and Textor's Cross-Polity Survey for the Ranking of Nations," *Social and Economic Studies,* **16,** 1967.

Farace, Vincent, and Donohew, Lewis. "Mass Communication in National Social Systems: A Study of 43 Variables in 115 Countries," *Journalism Quarterly,* **42,** 1965.

Russett, B. M., *et al. World Handbook of Social and Political Indicators.* New Haven, Conn.: Yale University Press, 1964.

Sawyer, Jack. "Dimensions of Nations: Size, Wealth, and Politics," *American Journal of Sociology,* **73,** 1967.

INDEX

Accuracy of theories, 17, 20
Alford, R. R., 32
Alker, H. A., 48, 62n, 69n
Allardt, E., 33, 37, 54, 55n, 69, 106n
Allport, G. W., 34n
Almond, G. A., 5n, 27n, 28, 33, 34n, 44, 48, 98n, 104n, 118
Amhavaara, Y., 130n
Analysis of variance, 77
Anderson, G. L., 53n
Anderson, H. H., 53n
Apter, D., 5n
Aron, R., 5, 6
Aronson, E., 101
Asch, S., 70
Automatic interaction detector, 36

Bauman, Z., 4, 53n
Bendix, R., 9, 26n, 42, 48n, 54n
Blalock, A., 32n
Blalock, H. M., 32n, 59n, 60n
Boudon, R., 69n
Braibanti, R. J., 23n
Brodbeck, M., 101n
Burnham, W. D., 49n
Bush, R. R., 11n, 93n

Campbell, A., 94n
Campbell, D. T., 103
Cantril, H., 33, 99, 118
Carnap, R., 76n
Cattell, R. B., 54, 56n, 122, 123
Causality of theories, 23
Chambers, W. N., 49n
Coefficient of context, 71
Coleman, J. S., 70

Collazo, J., 99n
Common indicators, 114, 115, 119
Composition rules, 101
Concomitant variation, 32, 35
Constructs, 100n
Converse, P. E., 44, 45n, 78n, 79, 94n
Correlational control of meaning, 124
Coser, L. A., 26n, 45n, 78n
Counterfactual statements, 25
Covariance, 59, 62, 63
Criterion validity, 96
Curvilinear relationships, 69, 71, 78
Cuzzort, R. P., 60

D'Andrade, R. G., 52n
Dawson, R. E., 49n
Degrees of freedom, 81, 83, 84
Developmental assumptions, 4
Discriminant validity, 103
Dogan, M., 33, 48
Domain of a concept, 94, 95, 108
Duncan, B., 60
Duncan, O. D., 60
Dupeux, G., 44, 45n, 78n, 79

Eckstein, H., 5n
Ellipticalness of theoretical and historical statements, 29
Error, 77, 102
Experimental design, 27, 38
Explanatory statements, 75, 76
Extrinsic system factors, 13

Face validity, 102
Factor analysis, 127
Factor congruence, 129

151

Factor loadings, 127, 128
Factor structures, 128, 129
Feierabend, I. K., 50
Feierabend, R. L., 50
Fiske, D. W., 103n
Fishbein, M., 128n
Frey, F. W., 34n

Galanter, E., 11n, 93n
Galton's problem, 51, 52
Galtung, J., 77n
Generality of concepts, 80
Generality of theories, 17, 21
Gilbert, G. M., 53n
Goodman, L. A., 60
Gottschalk, L., 5n
Grammar of measurement language, 97

Haas, M., 55n
Haller, A. O., 41n
Harmon, H. H., 129
Heidenheimer, A. J., 78n
Hempel, C. G., 19, 21, 23n, 25n, 76n
Hendin, H., 33n
Heyns, R. W., 69n
Historical generalization, 26
Hood, W. C., 23n
Hoselitz, B. F., 50
Huntington, S. P., 49, 55
Hyman, H., 34n

Identical indicators, 119
Incomplete determination, 7
Indicators, 95
Inference Rules, 101
Inkeles, A., 41, 45n, 125
Institutional setting factors, 54, 55
Interaction detection, 77
Interactive effect, 82
Interchangeability of measurement
    statements, 109, 110
International studies of values in politics,
    50, 124, 127
Interval scales, 99
Interval size, 111
Intrinsic system factors, 12
Ishino, I., 41n
Isolated system of variables, 23, 26

Jacob, P. E., 34n, 50n
Janowitz, M., 48

Kahl, J. A., 45n
Kaplan, B., 41n, 114n
Kendall, P. L., 56n
Kerlinger, F. N., 107n
Koopmans, T. C., 23n
Kornhauser, W., 64, 65n, 66
Kotarbinska, J., 22n
Kula, W., 53n
Kuroda, Y., 96n

Lazersfeld, P. F., 51n, 54, 56n
Least square solutions, 59
Levinson, D., 41
Levi-Strauss, C., 53
Lewis, D. I., 41n
Liepelt, K., 48n
Linear regression, 58
Lindzey, G., 101n
Lipset, S. M., 5n, 26, 33n, 42, 48n, 55, 95n
Lowie, R. H., 5n
Luce, R. D., 11n, 93n
Lunt, P. S., 96n

McClelland, D. C., 95n
Macridis, R. C., 5n
Maclay, H., 45n

Magnitude models of measurement, 100
Malewski, A., 7
Marx, K., 55, 65
Meade, R. D., 111n
Melikian, L. H., 49n
Meritt, R. L., 44, 51n, 106n
Merton, R. K., 5n
Meyerhoff, H., 5n, 6
Milbrath, L. W., 43, 44n
Miller, W. E., 94n
Modal personality, 41
Models of measurement, 93
Models of science, 3, 7, 8
Moore, W. E., 23n
Morris-Jones, W. H., 92n
Multidimensional concepts, 126, 127
Multiple regression model, 36
Munger, F. J., 32n

Nagel, E., 6, 76n
Naroll, R., 32, 51n, 52
Nominal scales, 98
Nowak, S., 18, 124n

Operational definition, 94
Ordinal scales, 98
Osgood, C. E., 11, 127, 128n
Ossowski, S., 9, 26n
Ostrowski, K., 78n
Overdetermination, 23, 34, 84

Parsimony of theories, 17, 21, 22
Partial correlations, 33
Pasamanick, B., 45n, 130n
Payaslioglu, A., 34n
Pesonen, P., 55n, 69
Pettigrew, T., 34n
Population contexts, 56
Population of indicators, 108, 109
Predictor validity, 114
Prothro, E. T., 49n
Przeworski, A., 78n, 124n

Radcliffe-Brown, A. R., 5n
Rae, D., 54, 55n
Ramsey, C. E., 99n
Regression coefficients, 58, 63
Regression intercept, 58
Regression of means, 60
Regression slopes, 60, 66, 68
Reification of concepts, 10
Reliability, 11, 95, 107, 115
Residual of variables, 25, 29, 30, 84, 132
Rettig, S., 45n, 130n
Robinson, W. S., 59, 60n
Rodd, W., 123
Rokkan, S., 33n, 48n, 51n, 54n, 55n, 106n
Rosen, B. C., 46
Rosenberg, M., 51n, 54, 56n
Rossi, P., 41n
Rules of inference, 20
Rules of interpretation, 93
Rummel, R. J., 51n, 55n
Russet, B. M., 69n, 94n

Samples of indicators, 109, 116, 117
Sampling, 31, 32

Scale origin, 111
Scott, W. A., 100n, 101n
Sears, R., 113, 114n, 117
Segal, D. R., 48n
Simon, H. A., 23n
Singer, J. D., 55n
Singer, M., 41n
Sjoberg, S., 11n
Skolimowski, H., 22n
Smelser, N. J., 5n, 11n
Smith, D. H., 45n, 125
Spengler, J. J., 23n
Spurious relationships, 63, 67, 72, 73, 82
Steiner, I., 128n
Stepwise multiple regression, 77
Stimulus equivalence, 108
Stokes, D. E., 94n
Structural contexts, 56
Structure of indicators, 117
Suchman, E. A., 9
Suci, G. J., 128n
Suppes, P., 11, 76n, 93n, 97n
Svalastoga, K., 33n
Systematic error, 98
Systemic factors, 35, 39, 40, 46
Systems, 10, 104, 105n

Tannenbaum, P. H., 128n
Tarski, A., 76n
Terhune, K. W., 86n
Teune, H., 34n, 50n, 124n, 127n
Thomas, E. M., 41n
Togerson, W. S., 98n

Validity, 11, 103, 106, 107, 114
Verba, S., 27n, 28, 33, 34n, 44, 48, 98n, 104n, 118

Walker, E. L., 69n
Ware, E. E., 45n
Warner, W. L., 96n
Watts, T. M., 34n, 50n
Wertheimer, M., 100n
Whittaker, J. O., 111n
Wiatr, J, J., 4
Wriggins, W. H., 4

Zinnes, J. L., 11n, 93n, 97